LEVERAGE

LEVERAGE

How to Get It and
How to Keep It
in Any Negotiation

ROGER VOLKEMA

AMACOM
American Management Association
New York • Atlanta • Brussels • Chicago • Mexico City •
San Francisco • Shanghai • Tokyo • Toronto • Washington, D.C.

> *Special discounts on bulk quantities of AMACOM books are available to corporations, professional associations, and other organizations. For details, contact Special Sales Department, AMACOM, a division of American Management Association, 1601 Broadway, New York, NY 10019.*
> *Tel.: 212-903-8316. Fax: 212-903-8083.*
> *Web site: www.amacombooks.org*

This publication is designed to provide accurate and authoritative information in regard to the subject matter covered. It is sold with the understanding that the publisher is not engaged in rendering legal, accounting, or other professional service. If legal advice or other expert assistance is required, the services of a competent professional person should be sought.

Library of Congress Cataloging-in-Publication Data

Volkema, Roger J.
　　　Leverage : how to get it and how to keep it in any negotiation / Roger Volkema.
　　　p.　cm.
　　　Includes bibliographical references and index.
　　　ISBN 0-8144-7326-1
　　　1. Negotiation in business.　I. Title.

HD58.6.V648　2006
658. 4'052—dc22

2005023210

© 2006 Roger Volkema.
All rights reserved.
Printed in the United States of America.

This publication may not be reproduced,
stored in a retrieval system,
or transmitted in whole or in part,
in any form or by any means, electronic,
mechanical, photocopying, recording, or otherwise,
without the prior written permission of AMACOM,
a division of American Management Association,
1601 Broadway, New York, NY 10019.

Printing number

　10　9　8　7　6　5　4　3　2　1

Contents

Acknowledgements — vii
Introduction — ix

1   Negotiation and Leverage — 1
2   Four Characteristics of Leverage — 7
3   The Four States of Leverage — 11
4   The Sources of Leverage — 15
5   Indicators of Leverage — 21
6   Checking Your Progress: Identifying Leverage — 33
7   Managing Leverage — 39
8   Increasing Your Leverage — 45
9   Decreasing the Other Party's Leverage — 55
10   Checking Your Progress: Altering Leverage — 67
11   The Dance of Leverage — 81
12   Reality Test — 87
13   Playing Defense — 93
14   The Climate of Negotiation — 109

15	Selecting an Approach	115
16	The Art of Communication	121
17	Another Reality Challenge	131
18	Leverage, Uncertainty, and Risk	137
19	Leverage and Ethics	143
20	Managing Emotions	151
21	Negotiating in Cyberspace	157
22	Multiparty Negotiations	161
23	International Negotiations	177
24	Surrendering Leverage	191
25	Final Thoughts	195

Resources	197
Appendix A—Mafia (An Intriguing and Useful Parlor Game)	199
Appendix B—Three-Party Negotiation	203
Index	209

Acknowledgments

This book is the result of contributions made by many individuals over the years—friends, colleagues, research assistants, and students. Many have contributed in ways in which they will never be aware, but to them I will always be grateful. Most specifically, I would like to thank Bob Wilson, Harry Webne-Behrman, Tom Sinclair, Fred Niederman, Patti Sinclair, Alison Torrillo French, Rob Jolles, Peter Trzyna, Cheryl Rivers, Joanne Miller, Ed Marod, and Brad Lyman for their careful reading of all or parts of earlier manuscripts. Their comments and suggestions led to countless improvements. A special thanks to Rob Jolles for once again serving as my mentor in negotiating the publication of this book. Thanks also to Ellen Kadin, my editor at AMACOM, who saw value in the concept of social leverage. Over the past few years, Mangal Kumar, Kimberly Kuchman, and Joanne Miller served as my research assistants, gathering anecdotes, summarizing research, and collecting data. And finally, to all the students with whom I have shared these and other ideas, models, questionnaires, and exercises, for their good humor and observations.

> I don't know what the future may hold
> but I know who holds the future.
>
> —RALPH ABERNATHY

INTRODUCTION

It is one of the hottest days of the year, and something is wrong with your refrigerator. The ice that had formed in the freezer section is melting. The temperature seems too warm. You contact a repairman, who promises to come that afternoon. You ask about the likely cost. He says it could be around $80. In the meantime, you keep both the refrigerator and freezer doors closed. The repairman arrives, late in the afternoon. He believes the problem is with your freezer. He takes out all the frozen foods, unscrews panels, cuts wires. There is the problem: A coil had gone bad. It will cost you $230.

Sound familiar? You are now at the mercy of the repairman. You know little to nothing about freezer coils, would have no idea where to get one, and all of your frozen foods are spread around the floor taking on room temperature. You have no choice and agree to pay the price.

This story has been repeated dozens of times in your life. If it wasn't the refrigerator repairman, it was the auto mechanic, the property tax assessor, or your employer. It was the owner of the home you wanted to buy, in a "sellers' market," or the sole supplier who wanted to double her prices. In each case, you felt at a disadvantage. You felt that you had little choice but to accede to the other party's demands. They had *leverage*.

The purpose of this book is to help you understand what leverage is, how you can increase your own leverage or decrease the leverage of another party, and the advantages and disadvantages of these approaches in all types of negotiations. Beyond helping you acquire a knowledge of leverage, this book offers questionnaires, exercises, and simulations to help you assess your strengths and weaknesses and to improve your skills in managing leverage in all types of negotiations: personal as well as professional. Negotiators of all experience levels will find the book useful and the concepts are illustrated with a variety of examples.

To some extent, this book is a follow-on to my earlier book on negotiation, *The Negotiation Toolkit*. It covers the more nuanced aspects of negotiating, particularly negotiating in difficult situations. However, you do not necessarily need to have completed that book, or any other book on negotiation, to gain value from this one. This book is self-contained and stands on its own.

As you can see from the table of contents, the book begins with an introduction to the fundamentals of leverage—what it is, the four states it can take, the sources of leverage, and the indicators or signals of leverage. Following completion of a questionnaire for measuring your skills in managing leverage, eleven techniques for changing leverage are presented in Chapters 8 and 9. The book progresses from two-party negotiations to more complex and specialized situations, including international and multiparty negotiations. Along the way, there are mini-cases to check your comprehension of the concepts (Chapters 6 and 10) and real negotiations to help you hone your skills (Chapters 12, 17, and 21).

The book is written in an interactive format and, for the most part, contains everything you need to assess your competencies and develop new skills in negotiation, though a pen or pencil will be helpful. The more opportunities you create for yourself to practice the techniques presented in the book, the more skilled you will become.

As you progress through the book, becoming more skilled in the ways of managing leverage, feel free to let me know about your experiences—triumphs, frustrations, discoveries, confusion, personal breakthroughs. I can be reached via e-mail at volkema@american.edu, and would be happy to respond to any questions or observations you may have.

1

> Wisdom consists of the anticipation of consequences.
>
> —**NORMAN COUSINS**

NEGOTIATION AND LEVERAGE

Negotiation is a social process that is central to our everyday existence. We are constantly negotiating in our personal and professional lives, often without realizing it. That is, we are communicating with others to determine the nature of future behavior—which restaurant to eat at, what movie to see, which supplier to hire, what price to offer, what work schedule to propose, and so on. In general, our overall well-being and livelihood are determined by how well we handle these varied situations.

We often think of negotiation as something that happens during a face-to-face encounter. In reality, negotiation is a more complicated, multistage process, beginning before most people realize it and continuing beyond the signing of an agreement (see Figure 1-1). How well these stages are managed determines the parties' satisfaction with both the process and the outcome.

In every negotiation, people feel some level of ease or discomfort, confidence or apprehension, and satisfaction or dissatisfaction, depending on the importance of the negotiation, time constraints, and one's negotiating counterpart. These feelings can occur in any of the stages of the negotiation process, including in anticipation of first encountering the other party (pre-negotiation), during face-to-face meetings and exchanges (introductions, information sharing, proposal surfacing), and when the contract or agreement is being executed. There are occasions, for example, when you feel at a distinct disadvan-

-1-

Figure 1-1. The negotiation process.

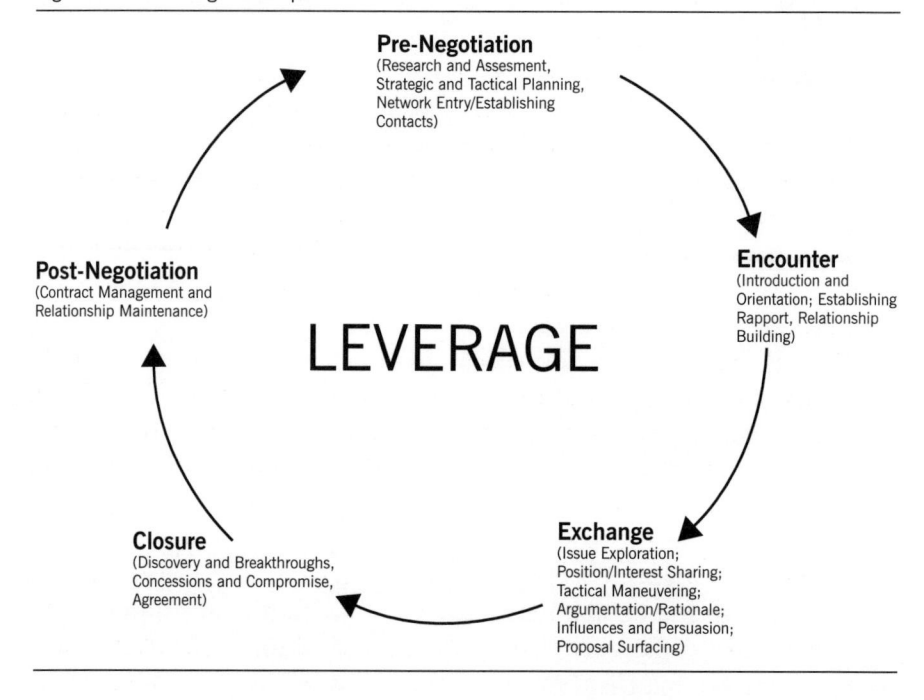

Pre-Negotiation
(Research and Assesment, Strategic and Tactical Planning, Network Entry/Establishing Contacts)

Encounter
(Introduction and Orientation; Establishing Rapport, Relationship Building)

Exchange
(Issue Exploration; Position/Interest Sharing; Tactical Maneuvering; Argumentation/Rationale; Influences and Persuasion; Proposal Surfacing)

Closure
(Discovery and Breakthroughs, Concessions and Compromise, Agreement)

Post-Negotiation
(Contract Management and Relationship Maintenance)

LEVERAGE

tage going into a negotiation, and the expectation becomes almost a self-fulfilling prophecy (like the refrigerator example in the introduction). On other occasions, an anticipated advantage or disadvantage will change during an encounter (for example, when you are offered a much better proposal than you expected). These feelings or sensations are the result of leverage.

Leverage Defined

Leverage is a word that is used in a number of different contexts, including finance, mechanics, and negotiation. In finance, for example, we hear about leveraged buyouts—the use of credit or debt to finance a company takeover, where the assets of the firm are used as collateral for the loans. In mechanics, people talk about using leverage to raise an object or pry something loose. Generally, mechanical leverage involves a fulcrum, like those that support teeter-totters or seesaws. More recently, the word *leverage* has been used liberally to describe almost any type of advantage, from leveraging the reputation of a product to leveraging customers, nutrition, culture, political discontent, and much more.

The origin of the word can be found in the context of mechanics. The root word of leverage is lever, which comes from the Middle English word *levour*. A *levour* was a bar used for prying or dislodging something, denoting the means of accomplishing a purpose. One of the characteristics of a lever is that it allows one not only to gain advantage, but to do so at a distance. According to the Oxford English Dictionary, the distance of the direction of a force from the axis (lever) is sometimes called the leverage of the force.[1]

This characteristic of leverage, derived from mechanics, can help us understand social leverage as well, and how it relates to power. Social leverage and power are similar in that both involve influencing the behavior of other parties. However, whereas power is often more obvious, proximate, and enduring (such as the legitimate power that comes from being the boss), leverage is frequently more subtle, and more effective when it is exercised from a distance. The more distance, the more leverage. In the biblical tale of David and Goliath, Goliath had power (mass, strength) but David with his slingshot had leverage.

Leverage in Action

Much like other social processes, such as love or hate or envy, leverage is difficult to measure. We do not have scales to determine how much love or hate we have for someone (although we talk about being green with envy, which may be the beginning of a color-based scale). However, in negotiation there is a qualitative measure of social leverage determined by the costs involved in failing to reach an agreement. It is the principal means of understanding leverage, including how to acquire it and how to change it. Social leverage is determined as follows:

The more it costs Party B not to have an agreement with Party A, the more leverage Party A has.

In the 1940s, a well-known actress and figure skater named Sonja Henie was making a movie called *Sun Valley Serenade*, produced by Darryl Zanuck. She had a contract stipulating that filming would end by a particular date. When that date came and went, an additional day of shooting was still needed. Henie refused to complete the film unless she was paid $200,000 (an exorbitant sum of money in those days, particularly for one day's work). The studio could not afford to scrap the movie, having already filmed nearly all of it. They had to have an agreement with Sonja Henie, and consequently she had substantial leverage and got the money.

Several years ago the pilots of a major airline were striking for better pay. The union called for wildcat strikes, which means that the pilots would refuse to fly planes at the last minute. With such short notice, it was impossible to get replacement pilots. Imagine your surprise and anger as a passenger when an airline representative announces that the plane you are about to board will not be flying after all . . . and there may or may not be another available flight. Would you want to fly that airline again any time soon? The costs to the airline of not reaching an agreement with the pilots' union were tremendous. In other words, the pilots had leverage.

When the United States wanted to invade Afghanistan after the September 11th disaster, there was one country from which it could have easy access—Pakistan. Pakistan is adjacent to Afghanistan, not only providing easy access for military operations but also providing potential sanctuary for Al Qaeda forces. The latter could be shut off, or at least minimized. The costs to the United States of not reaching an agreement with Pakistan were substantial. Therefore, Pakistan had leverage.

Sometimes leverage is memorialized through a common understanding, custom, or agreement. For example, there is a general understanding that journalists' sources will remain anonymous. If this were not the case, a source could suffer personal or professional calamity. One of the best illustrations of this was Deep Throat, the nickname that journalists Bob Woodward and Carl Bernstein gave to W. Mark Felt, their source of information about the Watergate affair. Woodward and Bernstein's investigation led to President Richard Nixon's resignation. Without the assurance of anonymity, Deep Throat would have been risking political suicide by leaking inside information. However, sources have leverage because any breech of this professional code would likely cause information to dry up for all journalists.

As these examples suggest, the costs of not having an agreement can range far and wide. A cost can be monetary, as it was for the movie studio faced with not being able to complete the film starring Sonja Henie. But costs can take many other forms, including time, reputation, face, friendship, tradition, psychological well-being, and opportunities. There may be multiple costs at stake, as in the case of the airline whose pilots were striking for better pay. If the pilots' union called a wildcat strike, the airline would not only incur an immediate loss of revenue but would also lose some measure of reliability and goodwill with prospective passengers.

Understanding leverage involves understanding costs. If there are multiple costs, then each cost must be understood in turn: What is the cost? What is its source? And what is its importance or relevance to a party? Sometimes a party perceives a cost where none really exists, or sometimes the costs can change. It is essential to understand the characteristics of costs (and leverage) if you want to manage leverage effectively and reach satisfactory agreements.

Note

1. To help you visualize the concept of distance, imagine being on a seesaw. If you sit close to the fulcrum, your feet will touch the ground (so the distance your force moves downward is minimal). In this position, you probably cannot lift someone sitting on the opposite end of the seesaw (unless they are very light). If you move to the end of the seesaw, however, the distance your body (force) travels up and down is much greater. At the top, your feet are dangling. But you have a better chance of lifting and controlling someone on the other end, particularly if they are sitting closer to the fulcrum. Thus, the distance of a force downward is greatest at the end of a long axis or lever, and that corresponds to leverage.

2

> Not believing in force is the same as not believing in gravitation.
>
> —LEON TROTSKY

FOUR CHARACTERISTICS OF LEVERAGE

In applying leverage, there are four important characteristics to understand. Leverage is: (1) based on perceptions, (2) dynamic, (3) situation specific, and (4) a social construct.

1. Leverage is based on perceptions.

If a party to a negotiation has an advantage and nobody perceives that the advantage exists (including the person with the advantage), then there is no leverage. This is especially true for the party with the disadvantage. If he does not perceive any costs to not having an agreement, then it is difficult for the other party to exercise an advantage. Thus, it is *perceived* cost, real or imaginary, that enables leverage.

Consider the following scenario. You and your spouse are planning to spend the weekend in an expensive honeymoon suite to celebrate your tenth wedding anniversary. At the last minute, your babysitter calls in sick. No one else seems available, as this is the last holiday weekend of the summer. As a last ditch effort, you contact a babysitter you employed several years ago, who is now in college. She also has plans for the weekend, but you feel you must try to "buy her out of them." While you are engaged in this negotiation, unbeknownst to you, your spouse has arranged for a family friend to take care of your daughter over the weekend.

Although there is no real cost to you of not reaching an agreement (since your spouse has found a babysitter), there is a tremendous perceived cost of not reaching an agreement with the former babysitter. Therefore, the former babysitter has leverage.

Perception is everything in negotiation, and leverage is based on perception. Consequently, retail stores will sometimes put only one or two of a particular item on a shelf, despite having ample stock in the back room, to suggest that it is popular and the store is down to its last few. This creates the perception that there are costs involved in delaying your decision: Buy now if you want one of these, because there are only a few left.

2. Leverage is dynamic.

Leverage can change quickly as new information becomes available. For example, while negotiating with the former babysitter, should you receive a call on your cell phone from your spouse, informing you that a family friend can babysit during your anniversary weekend, your perceived costs of not reaching an agreement would likely diminish substantially.

The fickle nature of leverage was most evident in an episode of the sitcom *Seinfeld* about the owner of a takeout soup establishment. Brilliant but temperamental, the proprietor is known as the "Soup Nazi." Customers are expected to follow a precise routine when ordering soup, or risk being scolded and banned from the restaurant. Everyone obeys his orders, because his soup is out of this world. Elaine, however, on a first visit, irritates him and gets banned. Through a fortuitous chain of events, she ends up with the Soup Nazi's family armoire, which has all his family's recipes for the soups. As the episode ends, Elaine is back at his restaurant, flaunting the recipes and, in effect, threatening his livelihood. The leverage has changed dramatically.

These sorts of changes occur during formal business negotiations as well. If, for example, information central to an upcoming bidding process known only to one company becomes available to other companies, then leverage among the companies has shifted. Leverage can also change if the needs or financial resources of one or more companies change, if the issues in the negotiation are altered (for example, the value of the contract on which the companies are bidding is substantially increased), or if new players enter the negotiation (for example, a new company with deep pockets joins the bidding process).

It is generally accepted that "knowledge is power," and nowhere is this more true than in managing leverage. Information is the lifeblood of negotiation. The more information that you have about the other party's needs or about the availability of additional resources or options, the stronger your negotiating position.

3. Leverage is situation specific.

In the preceding example, the former babysitter had leverage over the couple in need of a last-minute replacement. If, however, the babysitter was in need of a reference for a job application, the couple could suddenly have leverage. Likewise, the aforementioned company with privileged information might have an advantage over another company, but in another situation the advantage could be reversed (for example, the second company has just made a technical breakthrough that will revolutionize the industry).

Sometimes the situations that create leverage overlap, or can be linked in some way. A junior account executive at an advertising firm, knowing that her position is less than essential to the company, may lack leverage when asking for a raise. However, if an important ad campaign must be managed over the weekend and she is the only one available, then in this situation she has leverage. Further, she might try to link her availability and dependability in the future to securing a raise.

4. Leverage is a social or relational construct.

Therefore, one has advantage over another individual only as long as the relationship exists. If one party leaves the relationship (that is, transfers, resigns, separates), leverage ceases to exist. This characteristic is apparent when a husband and wife divorce and to some extent when a son or daughter becomes a legal adult and moves out of the house (gaining scheduling, dietary, and social freedoms). In university settings, when a dean steps down and assumes a position alongside the teaching faculty, the dean's "means of accomplishing a purpose" or leverage quickly diminishes. Without another party, it is like being on a seesaw by yourself.

An Illustration

All four characteristics of leverage were illustrated in a *Wall Street Journal* article, in a story about a pharmaceuticals executive named Michael

Valentino.[1] Mr. Valentino, who had worked for several drug companies during his career, was represented by a lawyer in his employment contract negotiations with the company that wanted to hire him as its CEO. The lawyer had built his reputation on winning attractive employment packages for his clients, and it was his job to get the best employment contract possible (salary, stock options, health benefits, golden parachute, etc.). To Michael Valentino, this may have appeared to be a difficult negotiation, because he had no track record with the new company. Further, since the person negotiating on behalf of the company had more information about other candidates for the position and about the company's financial resources and liabilities, Valentino may have perceived that he had little leverage. His lawyer, however, recognized that the hiring company had made the mistake of putting its general counsel in charge of the negotiations. Near the conclusion of the negotiations, in which he was able to get a very generous package for his client, he pulled Michael Valentino aside and said: "I knew from Day One we were going to get you everything you wanted. When this is over, you're going to be that guy's boss. He knows that. He can't fight you too hard on anything."

The perception of who had an advantage in this negotiation changed, albeit with the help of an agent. And the new perceived leverage was based on the relationship that the two principals would soon have—boss and subordinate—a relationship that was undeniable for the general counsel (unless he was planning to quit). Within the employment-contracting context, Michael Valentino gained leverage as the costs to the general counsel of not reaching an amicable agreement on the employment package became apparent. In another context, such as assuring that the company and its new CEO avoid some legal entanglements brewing with a government regulatory agency, the general counsel might be in a unique position to exercise an advantage.

Recognizing these four characteristics of leverage will help you to manage the negotiation process and, in particular, to alter leverage during a negotiation. Before we get into some specific techniques for accomplishing this, let's examine the four states of leverage that are possible due to the perceptual aspect of leverage.

Note

1. G. Anders, "Upping the Ante: As Some Decry Lavish CEO Pay, Joe Bachelder Makes it Happen," *Wall Street Journal*, June 25, 2003.

3

The eyes are not responsible when the mind does the seeing.

—PUBLILUS SYRUS

THE FOUR STATES OF LEVERAGE

Because leverage is based on perceptions, it is conceivable that one, both, or neither party in a negotiation can perceive a party's advantage. This creates differing degrees of advantage. The four states are: Active leverage, Blind leverage, Potential leverage, and Unknown leverage.

Active Leverage

If both the advantaged party in a negotiation and the disadvantaged party recognize the potential costs to the disadvantaged party of not reaching an agreement, the leverage can be described as Active leverage (Figure 3-1). The case of the malfunctioning refrigerator described in the introduction of this book is a good example of Active leverage. It is one of the hottest days of the year, the repairman has disassembled your freezer (now lying on the floor in pieces), and your frozen foods are beginning to thaw. The repairman (Party A in Figure 3-1) has Active leverage. He can readily perceive the costs to you (Party B) of not agreeing to his asking price, and you are acutely aware of your disadvantage.

Blind Leverage

It is also possible, however, for the disadvantaged party to recognize the costs involved in not reaching an agreement, although the advantaged party is not aware of his or her advantage. This is called Blind

Figure 3-1. Four states of leverage (for party A).

	Party A	
	Advantage Perceived	Advantage Unperceived
Party B — Disadvantage Perceived	Active Leverage	Blind Leverage
Party B — Disadvantage Unperceived	Potential Leverage	Unknown Leverage

leverage. In the movie "Being There," Peter Sellers played a simpleton named Chauncey Gardiner, who has little to say but whose utterances about gardening are taken as sage metaphors of economic analysis by powerful businessmen and politicians. Chauncey Gardiner has influence or leverage based on misperceptions of his analytical skills, even though he is blind to this advantage. Similarly, if you were to ask a repairman to stop by and look at your refrigerator, without specifying the exact nature or urgency of your situation, the repairman would have Blind leverage.

As these two examples suggest, Blind leverage has potency. As long as one party perceives he is at a disadvantage and could suffer significant losses from not reaching an agreement, the other party has leverage. This happens occasionally in a card game, such as poker. Playing with a novice, a more skilled poker player may want to fold with a poor hand (for example, a pair of fours) because she cannot be sure that the nonchalance of her adversary is based on strength or ignorance. If the bidding continues, the costs could get too high, so she folds or calls.

Blind leverage has its risks, however. Often the party with the perceived disadvantage will probe the other party to see if he is aware of the advantage. For example, in a game of poker, a party with a poor hand may try to bluff, raising the stakes dramatically to suggest to the other party that it will take a strong hand to win. In the case of Chauncey Gardiner, the physician who examined Chauncey for a leg injury was able to ascertain Chauncey's true level of intelligence. Had he been able to convince others that Chauncey's world of experience was limited to gardening and television, the Blind leverage would have evaporated.

The disadvantaged party, of course, could try to hide or limit his costs. For example, in the case of a malfunctioning freezer, you might ask a neighbor to store your frozen foods in their freezer. If you can only store items there for a day or two, or if you need to have everything working soon because you have relatives arriving for a visit, the repairman might not know the extent of your costs.

Potential Leverage

If the advantaged party perceives her advantage, but the disadvantaged party does not perceive the costs of failing to reach an agreement, the leverage is called Potential leverage. When you call the refrigerator repairman to describe the problem that you are experiencing with your refrigerator, he may immediately recognize the cause and severity of the problem. This gives him Potential leverage. Likewise, a scriptwriter who knows she has written a great screenplay has Potential leverage when approaching a producer or studio executive. So does a suitor with two tickets to a sold-out concert when he asks a love interest for a date, or a freight company executive approaching a potential client, knowing that his chief competitor is about to be shut down by a labor strike. David had Potential leverage over Goliath.

There are, in fact, many situations that might be characterized as involving Potential leverage. The art of diplomacy involves transforming Potential leverage into Active leverage—that is, into a situation where the disadvantaged party understands the costs of failing to reach agreement—without creating leverage for the other party in the process. Sometimes this is accomplished by leaking information through a third party, while other times the advantaged party will find a subtle way to reveal this information himself or herself. Simply by taking your freezer apart and revealing the burned-out coil, the repairman moves the leverage from Potential to Active. He doesn't have to say much.

Another way that Potential leverage is transformed into Active leverage is through the use of a "sweetener." With this tactic, a party will hold back one item during a negotiation, to be offered near the end of the negotiation to help close the deal. For example, as you teeter on a decision regarding the purchase of a new bicycle, the salesperson offers to throw in a protective cover for the bike. This item or offer sweetens the deal to the point of making it irresistible. The sweetener (an advantage known to the party making the gesture) represents one more cost to the other party of not reaching an agreement, a disadvantage that the other party is unaware of until the final, critical stage of the negotiation. The refrigerator repairman offering a two-year guarantee on parts and labor as you are hesitating to decide whether to go ahead with the costly repair would constitute a sweetener.

Unknown Leverage

Finally, it is possible that neither the advantaged party nor the disadvantaged party recognizes the situation. This is referred to as Unknown leverage. Unknown leverage is an unstable state, as there are always perceived costs in not reaching an agreement. Sometimes they surface naturally, and sometimes perceived costs are manufactured by one of the parties. For example, you are with a friend who is shopping for a new television. You are not in the market for a television, and are wandering about the store when you happen upon a display of Palm Pilots. Several friends at work have these. At about this time, a sales clerk asks if she can help you. You say thanks, but you are just looking. She lets you know that these are on sale today only, reduced 40 percent. Suddenly, there is a potential cost to you of not reaching an agreement. Similarly, if the refrigerator repairman in the previous example could repair other items without charging you for another house call, and your garbage disposal has recently experienced an occasional problem, this would represent Unknown leverage for the repairman.

Generally speaking, leverage moves from being Unknown to Potential or Blind leverage, and from Potential or Blind to Active leverage. How this happens is explained in the next chapter.

4

> Necessity never made a good bargain.
> —BENJAMIN FRANKLIN

THE SOURCES OF LEVERAGE

If leverage is determined by the perceived costs incurred by a party in not reaching an agreement, what, then, determines these costs?

Prior to any negotiation, certainly any important negotiation, an individual is advised to ask three fundamental questions. These are:

1. What do I want?
3. Why should the other party negotiate with me?
4. What are my alternatives?

Consciously or subconsciously, the parties ask themselves these questions. Your answers to the first question ("What do I want?") and the third question ("What are my alternatives?") determine how much leverage the other party has—Blind leverage, to be precise. If you want something very specific, you want it very badly, and you believe there is no substitute for this item, then the cost to you of not reaching an agreement is very high. Consequently, the other party has considerable leverage, particularly if your desire and lack of alternatives are recognized.

A friend's experience trying to buy an X-Men action figure several years ago provides an illustration. At a time when X-Men were all the rage, my friend went on a quest for one particular superhero named Magneto. His girlfriend's son wanted this action figure for Christmas. But then so did everyone else's child. In what seemed like the last store

– 15 –

on earth, my friend arrived just in time to be told by a clerk that the last one had been sold to the woman in front of him. Naturally he pleaded his case with this woman, hoping she would sell him Magneto, even if it meant paying two or three times what she had just paid for it. Because he desperately wanted this particular action hero and felt there were no other stores that might carry it, the woman had tremendous leverage.

In February 1504, Christopher Columbus and his crew were grounded in Jamaica, where the island natives had refused to continue to provide them with food (in part because of the abuses of Columbus). Consulting an almanac, Columbus saw that a lunar eclipse would occur on the last day of the month. On that day, he called the native chiefs to a meeting and told them that god would punish their people if they did not supply his crew with food. As an indicator of god's wrath, the moon would darken. The natives refused. Columbus retired to his ship for about an hour, just as the eclipse began. He returned just before the eclipse was to end, at the pleading of the natives. They were suddenly more than willing to provide Columbus and his crew with food. The moon and the sun were important to their culture and, indeed, their livelihoods. The natives not only wanted and needed these celestial bodies, but they knew of no alternatives to them. And Columbus appeared to be the only one who could control the moon.

Finally, consider the following situation. A nonprofit organization holds its annual carnival every February at a local hotel. In its twentieth year, the event now draws over a thousand people dressed in costumes, dancing to samba music all night long. For the past ten years the carnival has been held in this particular hotel, which is the only hotel in the area that can accommodate so many revelers. Last year, however, the hotel was sold. When representatives from the nonprofit organization approached the hotel's new management in November, they discovered that the hotel's fee for this ballroom had nearly doubled. With only three months before the event, and no known facility in the area that could hold a thousand people, the nonprofit organization reluctantly agreed to pay the higher fee.

You might recognize that these two questions—"What do I want?" and "What are my alternatives?"—are related to perhaps the two most recognizable concepts of economics: supply and demand (Figure 4-1). What a party wants constitutes his or her demand, based on real and perceived needs. The stronger a party's need or desire, the stronger

The Sources of Leverage

Figure 4-1. Fundamental questions and leverage.

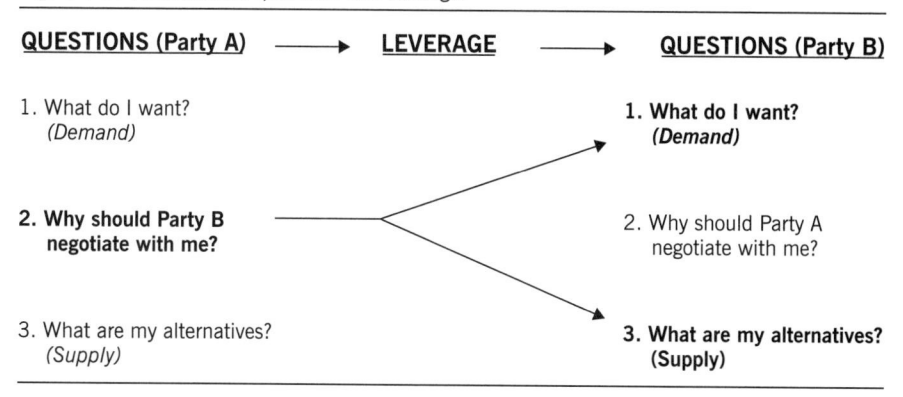

QUESTIONS (Party A)	→ LEVERAGE →	QUESTIONS (Party B)
1. What do I want? *(Demand)*		1. What do I want? *(Demand)*
2. Why should Party B negotiate with me?		2. Why should Party A negotiate with me?
3. What are my alternatives? *(Supply)*		3. What are my alternatives? *(Supply)*

the demand. And while the examples just offered focus more on material or substantive needs (for example, Magneto), an individual's desires can include psychological and relational needs as well.[1]

The alternatives available represent supply. The smaller the supply of an item, the fewer alternatives a party has available to acquire the item. Thus, my friend in search of the X-Men action hero had a strong demand for something in short supply (Magneto), which gave the woman who had bought the last one plenty of leverage. Likewise, there is only one moon, and only one person who appeared to the Jamaican natives able to control it—Columbus. And the nonprofit organization apparently had only one local hotel that could accommodate its annual event.

While it might appear from many of these examples that only one party can have leverage in any given situation, this is not the case. Because leverage is based on perceptions, if both parties fail to perceive that they are at a disadvantage, then neither side has leverage. However, quite the opposite is also possible, that both sides perceive a disadvantage.

For example, a property management firm (Party A), desperate for an unusual size refrigerator to go in its new apartment complex that is soon to open, contacts what it believes is the only refrigerator manufacturer that can help it (Party B). Unbeknownst to the property management firm, the refrigerator manufacturer has been stuck with several thousand of these unusual refrigerators as a result of a prospective buyer's bankruptcy. The manufacturer, not aware of the property management firm's situation, believes this may be its only opportunity to clear inventory. In this case, each party believes the other has considerable leverage (Blind leverage, as shown by Point X in Figure 4-2).

This can change, of course, as the parties exchange information. If the property management firm were to communicate its desperate need for this special refrigerator, which it has not been able to find anywhere else, the refrigerator manufacturer's (Party B's) leverage would become Active (Point Y in Figure 4-2). If the refrigerator manufacturer were to attempt to reinforce the property management firm's predicament (for example, by emphasizing the time constraint or scarcity of refrigerator manufacturers), the refrigerator manufacturer could actually strengthen its Active leverage (Point Y'). If, on the other hand, the refrigerator manufacturer were to reciprocate and reveal that it had gotten stuck with several thousand of these refrigerators, which no one else can use, the property management firm's leverage would become Active as well (Point Z in Figure 4-2).

The ideal set of states for each party is shown by the triangles in Figure 4-2. Party A's ideal situation, for example, is to have Active leverage while the other party has Unknown leverage or at most Potential/

Figure 4-2. Degrees of leverage for parties A and B in a negotiation.

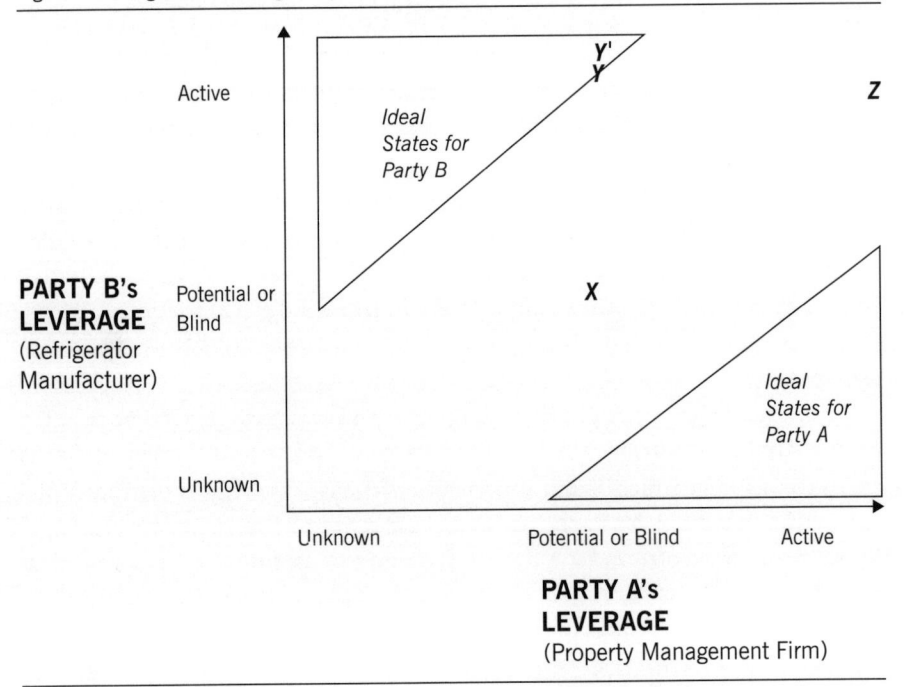

Blind leverage, or to have Potential/Blind leverage while the other party has Unknown leverage.

The key to determining leverage in a negotiating situation is assessing your wants and needs (Question #1) and your alternatives (Question #3), which will help you understand and control the other party's perceived advantage, and to answer Question #2 ("Why should the other party negotiate with me?"). The answer to Question #2 is determined by the other party's perceived wants/needs and alternatives (that is, their answers to the first and third questions). These answers also can be managed.

How can you tell who needs whom? In the next chapter, we'll see how the basic indicators of leverage are associated with time, space, and behavior.

Note

1. Over the years, various scholars have sought to develop a universal model of human needs. One of the most widely recognized models is Abraham Maslow's needs hierarchy, which consists of five needs—physiological, security, affiliation, esteem, and self-actualization. The most fundamental or potent need in this hierarchy is the desire to satisfy physiological/survival needs through food, water, and shelter. Although Maslow's needs hierarchy has some general utility, it has been suggested that human needs likely vary depending on a number of factors, including culture. In many collectivist cultures, for example, such as found in Japan and China, it has been argued that the most potent need is not individual survival but rather social identity or belonging.

5

> Show business is tough . . . it's a dog-eat-dog world. No . . . it's worse . . . it's dog-doesn't-return-another-dog's phone call.
>
> —WOODY ALLEN

INDICATORS OF LEVERAGE

Because a negotiator's wants or needs and available alternatives are key to determining leverage, individuals will frequently withhold this information from their counterparts. Then, one is left to look for other signs or indicators of the other party's situation, while at the same time trying to conceal or disguise one's own condition.

There are many ways that this can be done, since there are many different indicators of leverage that can occur throughout the negotiation process. Table 5-1 lists seventeen common indicators, along with the stages in the negotiation process where they are most likely to appear— Pre-negotiation, Encounter, Exchange, Closure, and Post-negotiation (from Figure 1-1).

Since leverage is based on perceptions, understanding and managing these signals is crucial to controlling a negotiation. Each of these indicators is discussed in more detail below.

Initiating Contact

The mere act of one party contacting another suggests that the former believes the latter has something of value, something that isn't available elsewhere. When you go to a pawnshop to sell an item, the signal you are sending is that you are down to your last resort, that you have exhausted other sources of money (friends, relatives), and are quite desperate. You are willing to accept a fraction of the value of an item from the pawnbroker for this money.

Table 5-1. Indicators of leverage.

| | Stage of Occurrence |||||
Indicator	Pre-Negotiation	Encounter	Exchange	Closure	Post-Negotiation
1. Initiating Party		X	X		
2. Meeting Location	X	X	X	X	
3. Wait Time		X	X	X	X
4. Style of Dress		X	X	X	X
5. Gifts/Meals		X	X	X	X
6. Seating Arrangement		X	X	X	
7. Space/Posture		X	X	X	
8. Number of Associates/Confederates		X			
9. Touching/Eye Contact		X	X	X	
10. Language Spoken		X			
11. Titles/Position		X	X	X	
12. Order, Amount of Speaking		X	X		
13. Age	X	X			
14. Gender	X	X			
15. Appearance		X	X	X	X
16. Response Time/Persistence		X	X	X	X
17. Author of Agreement			X		

Note: These indicators reflect Western traditions and culture, and may vary in other regions of the world.

Some years ago, the owner of the Houston Astros major league baseball team, Drayton McLane, tried to lure six-time Cy Young award-winning pitcher Roger Clemens out of his recent retirement. McLane's pursuit of Clemens signaled that Clemens had leverage. As a consequence, Clemens was able to negotiate a special deal for himself, unprecedented in professional baseball: He was not required to travel with the team to their away games, instead staying in Houston to spend more time with his family.[1]

There is a dating service that brings together single people interested in meeting other singles. It is a very structured event involving a series of small-group chats throughout the evening with people who share similar interests, hobbies, love of animals, politics, and so on.

Indicators of Leverage

Each participant has five slips of paper onto which they write their phone numbers. If you meet someone during the evening you would like to get to know better, you write your name and something about yourself on the slip of paper, along with your phone number, and give it to the person. One friend told me that he received two slips from the same woman, an indicator that she found him interesting or desirable in some way (wants/needs) and that she did not see many other alternatives at the event.

At such an event, the people in the room are relatively easy to contact. This is not always the case. The more difficult it is to reach an individual (due to security personnel, constant busy signals, administrative interference, telephone interruptions, unreturned messages, and so on), and the more persistent the initiating party becomes, the stronger the indicator that the unreachable party has leverage. And as Woody Allen's quote about Hollywood suggests, people with leverage do not return phone calls, at least until they see a need to do so (that is, until they see how you can help them or hurt them).

The difficulty of reaching someone comes in many forms. Executives have lawyers. Actors and directors have agents, who often are lawyers. Roger Clemens had two agents. And they all have administrative assistants. The more layers that exist between you and the party you are trying to reach, the stronger the indicator that this individual is important and powerful. In other words, he has leverage in most situations, and where this is not necessarily the case, he wants to convey an advantage nonetheless. A sole proprietor that I know hired a woman with a British accent to record the message on his answering machine. You cannot reach him directly, but must use a three-digit extension for his telephone line. Indeed, there have been any number of television or big screen comedies where an individual in a small office, perhaps a sole proprietor, answers his own telephone in a different voice, pretending to be his own secretary screening calls. The purpose is to give the perception of leverage.

Meeting Location

If you have to travel to another party's home or office, chances are she has leverage. In the movie "The Wizard of Oz," Dorothy and her friends had to travel to Oz to gain an audience with the Wizard; he did not come to them. Because the Wizard was the only one who could help Dorothy, the Scarecrow, the Tin Man, and the Cowardly Lion with their problems, they had no alternative. At least that was their perception. Similarly, if you want an audience with the Pope, you are best advised to go to the Vatican. Doctors make few if any house calls any more; you have to go to their offices. The same is true for lawyers. (Hopefully, we will never see the day when refrigerator repair people stop making house calls.)

Thus, when someone in a position of greater authority or prestige comes to you, it is probably an indicator that you have considerable leverage. The dean of a business school, for example, who had gained some reputation for his school, was approached by a headhunter about his interest in a vacancy at another university. The dean said that he was not interested in competing for another position, but if the president of the university wanted to offer him the job, he was willing to listen. The next day, the president of the university arrived by private plane. Who do you think had more leverage?

Wait Time

Once you get to the other party's home or office, you must then contend with wait time. People who have the leverage to make you come to them are busy people. They have other business options, and they let you know this by making you wait outside their offices. The same administrative assistants who kept you from making the appointment in the first place are there to tell you when their boss is ready to see you. This includes doctors, mechanics, executives . . . anyone who has a waiting room. Even when they call you, the party with leverage often makes you wait: "Mr. Myers, I have Victor Massey on the line for you. Will you please hold for Mr. Massey?" After some pause, Mr. Massey comes on the line.

Sometimes they won't allow you back to their office. You will be escorted to a conference room, where you may meet briefly before being turned over to an assistant. Or they will come out to the front desk to meet with you, perhaps without the courtesy of asking you to sit down, an indicator that you have no perceived leverage and that you will be accorded minimal time and attention.

People with leverage also are more likely to cancel meetings. It is not uncommon for individuals who perceive that they have other, better options than meeting with you to agree to an appointment but ask for your phone number in case they have to cancel. Don't be surprised if their assistant calls to cancel. Then, you have to be the initiator to try to reschedule the meeting, which further signals their leverage.

Style of Dress

Individuals who perceive themselves to be at a disadvantage in a negotiation often will dress more formally to impress the other party and bring gifts to ingratiate themselves with the other party. More formal attire, for example, is common among individuals going to job fairs and to company job interviews; they dress to demonstrate respect and to suggest competence.

Attire is not a straightforward indicator of disadvantage, however. A prospective employee, knowing that he has all the skills required for a position, and that no one else can fulfill this role, might signal his awareness of this advantage by dressing down for the interview. By dressing casually, the prospective employee is saying that he knows he has leverage. That is, the leverage is Potential or Active rather than Blind. This can be dangerous, however, if the leverage is only Potential (the advantage known to the prospective employee but not perceived by the interviewer). The interviewer may interpret the candidate's attire as a sign of disrespect or inexperience, and never give the candidate an opportunity to demonstrate his unique skills or talents.

An agent dressing in expensive clothes and jewelry is likely to suggest competence and success (that is, that the agent can help you solve your problem or get what you desire, as she has time and again for other clients). A private consultant once told me that buying one $3,000 suit dramatically improved his ability to get consulting jobs with major companies.

For some individuals, their offices are an extension of their attire. A large, well-appointed office communicates an ability to make things happen. And the photos taken with well-known people that hang on the wall also suggest competence and alternatives. Likewise, the use of highly sophisticated communication technology for conferencing and presentations suggests competence.

Gifts and Meals

Gifts also can signal leverage. Insurance and real estate agents, for example, are forever sending calendars, birthday cards, and holiday greetings. Many nonprofit organizations do the same, sending holiday stamps or greeting cards. Product representatives will offer prospective buyers everything from token gifts to expensive dinners to weekend retreats. These gifts suggest leverage for the other party.[2]

Similarly, the individual who buys lunch usually has less leverage. Frequently, for example, it is the salesperson or lobbyist who pays for lunch. In recent years, more and more financial retirement companies have offered free dinners to prospective clients. Time-share and other real estate companies have offered much more—lodging, appliances, vacations.

Seating Arrangement

At a meeting, seating arrangements can signal advantage. The power positions at a table are at the ends of the table and in the middle of the table. Pictures of the President of the United States, meeting with his cabinet at the White House, always show him sitting in the middle of the table and flanked by his cabinet members. In the television show "The Apprentice," Donald Trump sits in the middle of the large table with an associate on either side, facing the team of ambitious future executives competing for a position in his company.

Space and Posture

Individuals with power often occupy more space than others. In a meeting, this may be realized by empty chairs left on one or both sides of the individual. These individuals may physically take up more space by crossing their legs ankle-to-knee, by moving around (particularly if they have a chair that rocks or swivels), or by spreading out their materials on the table in front of them. They might lean back to create more distance between themselves and others, even staying behind their desk (a natural insulator). An individual addressing someone with perceived leverage might typically lean forward to close the distance, trying all the while to engage the other party.

In "The Apprentice," the business associates that sit on either side of Donald Trump leave enough space between themselves and their boss for another chair or two. Donald Trump's chair is physically larger than the chairs of his associates, and the associates' chairs are more plush if not larger than the chairs of the candidates. The high back on Trump's chair resembles a throne. Furthermore, his chair is some distance from the main door and with its back near a wall for support and, historically, protection. In this position, he can easily see others entering the room. And he exits through a private door at his back.

Number of Colleagues

Leverage is also signaled by the size of someone's entourage, partnership, or constituency. People with power have assistants, attendants, and admirers. At a boxing match, each fighter arrives with a number of supporters, assistants, and bodyguards surrounding him. The same is true for many rock stars. Recognizing that size matters, a private consultant will sometimes add the phrase "and associates" to the name of his or her firm. For example, a consultant named John B. Smith might name his firm "J.B. Smith and Associates" to suggest there are more partners or employees than just John Smith. Oliver North, on trial for the Iran-Contra scandal, created a constituency by wearing his U.S. military uniform at his trial. To convict him was, in essence, to indict the military and the country it protected. Similarly, celebrities such as O.J. Simpson and Michael Jackson have an advantage in a public trial because they have a constituency.

Touching and Eye Contact

Touching—related to the use of space—is another indicator of leverage. While there are cultural differences regarding touching and personal space, generally speaking, people with leverage are more likely to touch those lacking leverage than vice versa. In fact, there is an expression that captures the advantage gained in this way: "to put the touch on someone." It is harder to say no to a request accompanied by a touch. Politicians know this, so they kiss babies and "press the flesh." Try not voting for someone who shook your hand. And high-status people generally enjoy more touch liberties than their low-status counterparts.[3]

Often parties with leverage provide less eye contact (as they have other options to consider), and are more likely to be interrupted by phone calls (which they take) and to excuse themselves during your meeting to attend to other matters. By attending to interruptions they are effectively saying that either they do not believe you have something that is important to them, that they believe they can get what you are offering elsewhere, or both.

Language Spoken

When negotiations are international and the parties speak two different languages, the language of discourse may suggest which party has more leverage. This indicator is reinforced by other signs as well. For example, a fast-food chain is seeking to open franchises in a new market. They travel overseas (one indicator of leverage), meet prospective partners on their turf (a second indicator), and employ a translator to speak in the language of the other party (a third indicator).

Modes of Address

Leverage is also indicated in the way individuals address each other. Those lacking leverage may feel inhibited about initiating conversation with someone who has considerable perceived leverage. Madonna, for example, after her career had already been launched with hit songs such as "Like a Virgin," reports to being stunned when she first met former Beatle George Harrison, who she described as a real legend.

In cases of severe leverage differential, there may even be protocol established for controlling behavior. The Queen of England, for example, is someone who expects others to follow her lead, shaking hands if the queen offers a handshake, conversing if she is willing. Further, people with leverage are often referred to by a title: Mister, Doctor, Senator, President, Professor, Master, His Highness, His Holiness, Her Majesty, etc.

Order and Amount of Speaking

Who does the talking in a negotiation is another signal of leverage. In some situations, tradition determines the protocol (for example, following the Queen's lead). In many cases, however, it is the person perceived as lacking power (and with the greater need) who does most of the talking. He or she is often trying to capture and then maintain the other party's attention, since the other party is the one with less to lose if the negotiation fails. In fact, there is an old saying that he who speaks first loses. This implies that speaking first (and most) signals a greater perceived need, and thus that the other party has leverage.

Age

In some cultures, demographic characteristics such as age and gender signal leverage. In many East Asian cultures, for example, age is venerated. The young defer to the old, who are respected for their accumulated wisdom. A company founded in a Western culture, doing business in China for the first time, might not be aware of this custom. By sending a young representative, the company puts itself in a one-down position.

Gender

Similarly, gender can play a role in signaling leverage. In most cultures, women occupy a secondary role when it comes to business, if they play any role at all. Without question, this is changing. But in most Middle Eastern countries, for example, women do not engage in many forms of commerce. Even in the United States, women are limited by the proverbial "glass ceiling," the transparent barrier that historically has kept them from rising to executive positions. Thus, if a businessman encounters a woman counterpart in a negotiation, he may not offer the respect that he would give to a man.

Appearance

Appearance can signal, if not determine, leverage, with those deemed good looking often gaining an advantage. This was illustrated in an episode of the television news magazine "60 Minutes," through a staged event involving a broken-down automobile. The program filmed two different women who appeared to be having car problems along a busy roadway. The situations were identical, except one woman was exceptionally good looking. Who do you think got the most men to stop and offer assistance?

The influence of appearance in gaining an advantage has been demonstrated empirically in a number of studies. Individuals who are judged to be good looking are more likely to be given the benefit of the doubt in classrooms, courtrooms, the work environment, and in their own homes. They are more likely to be viewed by recruiters as being a good "fit" with the organization, so they are more likely to be hired and promoted. In fact, attractive people have been found to earn 5 to 10 percent more than others.

Response Time

The period of time a party demands to respond to a request or proposal can also suggest leverage. A potential buyer who asks to get back to you next week appears either not to be sold on what you are offering or is aware of alternatives that might be as good or better than your offer. In other words, this buyer apparently sees little in the way of costs to not having an agreement with you . . . or is a good bluffer hoping to see if a delaying tactic will cause you to tip your hand. And the more persistent you are, the more you validate the buyer's perception that you have little or no leverage.

This was the case in the movie "The Wizard of Oz," when Dorothy and her companions traveled some distance to Oz to ask the Wizard for a brain, a heart, courage, and passage back to Kansas, only to be told "The Wizard says 'go away.' " The fact that Frank Morgan played not only the Wizard in the movie, but most of the people between Dorothy and the Wizard (the Guardian of the Gate, the Cabbie, and the Palace Guard), and was himself the Palace Guard who said that the Wizard says to go away, only underscores the Wizard's astute awareness of putting personnel between himself and others as a demonstration of leverage.

Author of Agreement

Finally, there is the issue of who records the agreement. In most cases, the party with perceived leverage is the one to record the agreement. This allows them to put things in their own words, often with their own interpretation. And if the agreement is printed on high-quality paper with embossed lettering, already signed, it can be difficult for the party lacking leverage to suggest changes.

Multiple Indicators

Given all these indicators, imagine a worst-case scenario involving multiple indicators of leverage. After many attempts, you finally get an appointment with your negotiating counterpart. You have to travel some distance to meet in her office, but you must first wait outside the office until she will see you. She is older, and occupies a huge office with pictures of herself with famous people she has met throughout her life. She is busy, and your meeting is constantly interrupted. People come

Indicators of Leverage

in attending to her various needs—coffee, reports, and so on. She has honorary degrees, and goes by the title Doctor. Her eyes are constantly diverted, as if thinking about something else while you are meeting. After a short period, she thanks you for coming, extends her hand, and says someone will get back to you. Sound familiar?

You may have noticed in Table 5-1 that the Encounter stage has more indicators than any of the other stages. As is the case with many processes—problem solving, decision making, team building—the early stages often set the direction for succeeding stages. For example, how you formulate a problem will affect how you end up solving it. The same is true for negotiation. The early stages, particularly the Encounter stage, can affect all that follows. So it is important to recognize how leverage might be assumed or established in this stage.

While these factors are cues that suggest who has leverage and who does not, it is important to keep in mind that leverage is based on perceptions. Consequently, a skilled negotiator might try to fool you with one or more of these indicators (recall, once again, the Wizard from "The Wizard of Oz"). And you might try to do the same. Generally speaking, however, the more of these indicators that exist, the greater the perceived leverage.

Think about one of your most recent negotiations. Which of these indicators favored the other party having leverage? Which indicators favored you? Do you think this influenced the process and outcome of the negotiation? Since many of these indicators are under your control, you might want to experiment with altering one or more of these in the future (for example, the place you meet to negotiate with a prospective business associate). You may find that the dynamics of the negotiation change as well.

Notes

1. While there certainly was some player resentment to this deal, since everyone else had to travel to away games regardless of whether they were scheduled to play or not, Clemens pitched well enough to win a seventh Cy Young award and help the Astros make the playoffs.

2. Please note that in some cultures bringing gifts is common practice, not necessarily a signal of leverage. In fact, many of the indicators presented in this chapter represent what one might expect to find in North America, Northwestern Europe, Australia, and New Zealand. In

other cultures, some of these behaviors will occur naturally, not necessarily signaling an advantage. This will be discussed in more detail in a later chapter on international negotiations.

3. In an interesting study conducted by Brenda Major and Richard Heslin ("Perceptions of cross-sex and same-sex nonreciprocal touch: It is better to give than to receive." *Journal of Nonverbal Behavior*, 1982, 6, pp. 148–162), subjects were shown silhouettes of pairs of people facing each other, one touching the other's shoulder. The subjects judged the toucher to not only be more assertive, but of higher status.

6

> Experience is the name everyone gives to their mistakes.
>
> —Oscar Wilde

Checking Your Progress: Identifying Leverage

Now that you have a better sense of what leverage is, let's see how good you are at spotting it. Consider each of the three scenarios below. Identify which party has leverage, why you believe this to be the case, and whether the leverage is Unknown, Potential, Blind, or Active, as defined in Chapter 3. Use the indicators from the previous chapter to guide you in your identification.

Scenario A

Jack, an entrepreneur who works out of his home, is having problems with his computer. There appears to be a virus that has infected the word processing program. Two people have written to him that documents he has sent within the past two days have been flagged as having a virus. While one recipient was able to clean the virus and open the document, the other party does not want to risk infecting her computer. Although Jack has a virus-detection system in his computer, it has not been updated for some time, and he does not know how much it will cost to upgrade this system. Jack has a nephew, Michael, who knows a lot about computers, but Michael is out of town for five days. Jack cannot afford to wait five days; he has correspondence that must be sent out. He contacts the antivirus company using their 1-800 number, describes his situation, and learns that an upgrade will cost $250. He was hoping it would cost about $50.

1. Who has leverage? _____
2. Why do you believe this to be the case?_____

3. In what state is the leverage for the advantaged party (or parties)—Unknown, Potential, Blind, or Active? _____

In this case, the antivirus company has leverage. There are several indicators, most notably that Jack is contacting them about a problem. The costs to Jack of not having an agreement—of not getting rid of the virus once and for all—and soon are reasonably strong. He could lose goodwill and business if the problem isn't addressed. But the antivirus company's leverage is not overwhelming. This is because Jack has alternatives, both realized and potential alternatives. What are some of Jack's alternatives? They include: waiting for his nephew Michael (which he recognizes as a less-than-ideal alternative), renting or borrowing another computer until Michael returns, and identifying other antivirus system providers. In all likelihood, the leverage in this case is Active. Jack is disadvantaged, the antivirus provider has an advantage, and both are aware of the general circumstances.

Let's try another case, a bit more difficult.

Scenario B

A large residential development set to open in three weeks is in a jam. The grounds of the development, called Woodbrook, were designed and advertised to be among the most beautiful in the city. Unfortunately, the company that was to provide the watering system for the development, Tyler Systems, may not be able to fulfill its contract. While they have the labor force to install the tubing and sprinkler heads, and they have the sprinkler heads in stock, they may not be able to provide the special 4-cm. tubing due to a machine malfunctioning. This is an uncommon size tubing, although not completely unique to Tyler Systems. There is one other company that might be able to provide this tubing, MWB Ltd., but they are a major competitor of Tyler Systems. Consequently, Tyler is not likely to contact them for assistance. Unbeknownst to Woodbrook, MWB has a large stock of this special tubing. It was part of a special order for a proposed golf course that was being built in an adjacent county. But the developers of the

Checking Your Progress: Identifying Leverage

golf course declared bankruptcy shortly before the course was supposed to open, leaving MWB with nearly half of the 13,000 meters that the golf course had ordered . . . and no payment received. The residential development firm needs to have sod laid for the grand opening of the development in three weeks, but they must have the underground sprinkler system in before the sod is put down. Given Tyler Systems' reluctance to deal with MWB Ltd., the owners of Woodbrook have decided to take matters into their own hands and inquire.

1. Who has leverage? _____
2. Why do you believe this to be the case? _____
_____

3. In what state is the leverage for the advantaged party (or parties)—Unknown, Potential, Blind, or Active? _____
_____

This is a somewhat more complicated case. Remembering that the more it costs a party not to have an agreement, the more leverage the other party has, it would seem that the owners of the residential development are in a bind. They cannot postpone the grand opening of Woodbrook, and they have to have sod down for the opening. It is probably unreasonable to rent the sod, as later removal would likely lead to bad public relations. Therefore, in their minds, MWB Ltd. is the only company that can potentially help them. And when they contact MWB, they will of course discover that MWB has the very product they are looking for—4-cm. tubing. The fact that the residential development owners are initiating the call is one signal that the other party (MWB) has leverage.

In this case, however, MWB is also in a bind. They have been stuck with this special tubing due to a buyer's bankruptcy. If they cannot sell it to Woodbrook, they might never get rid of it (unless they can convince a future client that this special size is just what they need). It probably has little scrap value. And storage costs for this amount of tubing are significant. So when the owners of Woodbrook call, it will quickly become apparent that selling to Woodbrook is what they want (assuming Woodbrook will take most, if not all, of the tubing) and that they might not have an alternative.

As long as Woodbrook wants to remain committed to the proposed sprinkler system (and, in particular, the Tyler Systems sprinklers), Tyler

Systems has leverage. They have the sprinklers, not to mention the workforce to install them. And they likely have a contract as well, although if it was carefully reviewed by Woodbrook there will be a clause specifying the expected completion date and a penalty if that deadline is missed.

Interestingly, Woodbrook has leverage with MWB because MWB needs to get rid of the tubing. Unfortunately, it is Blind leverage. Once Woodbrook contacts MWB, MWB will have Active leverage. If MWB reveals that it has the tubing in stock, then Woodbrook's Blind leverage becomes Active leverage.

This scenario is a good illustration of how both parties can have leverage, and how leverage can change its state as the negotiation unfolds.

Here's one more scenario.

Scenario C

You are on your way to a meeting, driving alone through a commercial district. It is a cloudy day with the threat of rain in the air. You are driving within five or ten miles of the speed limit, listening to the radio. Traffic is a bit heavier than usual, but you do not mind; you have sufficient time to make your meeting. Suddenly the car in front of you comes to an abrupt stop. You slam on your brakes, but you cannot stop before hitting the car. You pull over and get out of your car to investigate the damage. There seems to be only minor damage to your car, but the car in front has significant damage to the bumper and taillight. You approach the other driver, who has gotten out of his car. He too is alone. You are upset because you know the law and you are at fault: You failed to stop in an assured clear distance. But you cannot understand why the driver of the other car stopped suddenly. Worse, you have a number of points on your driver's license and cannot afford another ticket. Not only would getting a ticket make your insurance go up, but it would put you closer to losing your license. Just then it begins to rain. You did not bring an umbrella, since you hadn't anticipated being outside for any length of time.

    1. Who has leverage? _____
    2. Why do you believe this to be the case? _____

Checking Your Progress: Identifying Leverage

3. *In what state is the leverage for the advantaged party (or parties)—Unknown, Potential, Blind, or Active?* _____

This may seem like an easy case to assess. It is going to cost you a lot not to reach an agreement with the other driver. If you can convince him to keep the police out of this, you may be able to avoid points and hold on to your license. You don't appear to have any alternative. You might presume that the other driver knows the law as well, and that you should have been following at a safer distance. Thus, the other driver probably has Active leverage.

Now imagine that the following develops.

The driver of the other car hurries over to you and asks to get into your car. You happily agree, since it is raining and you want to stay presentable for your meeting. Once you both are inside your car, you notice that the other driver has an odd, sweet smell about him. Then you recognize it. It is the smell of marijuana.

1. *Who has leverage?* _____
2. *Why do you believe this to be the case?* _____

3. *In what state is the leverage for the advantaged party (or parties)—Unknown, Potential, Blind, or Active?* _____

This changes things, doesn't it? Marijuana is illegal, and one certainly cannot drive under the influence of any illegal substance. The driver of the other car undoubtedly hurried to your car because he did not want you to discover that he was smoking marijuana. He, too, does not want the police involved. So now it appears that you have leverage, as it could cost the other driver dearly if the police were to be summoned. In fact, you have considerable leverage. When the accident occurred, your advantage was Blind. But at the point where the other driver becomes aware that you recognize what he has been smoking, the leverage turns Active.

What would you do at this stage? Would you say to the other party, "Hey, you've been smoking marijuana!"? How you move your advantage from Blind to Active can determine how effective you will be. We will look more closely at forms of communication in a later chapter. But next, let's explore the ways you can manage leverage.

7

> A man of action forced into a state of
> thought is unhappy until he can get out of it.
> —JOHN GALSWORTHY

Managing Leverage

As indicated earlier and illustrated in the last two scenarios, leverage is a dynamic social process based on perceptions. This means that during the course of a negotiation, leverage can change as perceptions change . . . and more than once. In some cases, there is actually an ebb and flow to perceived advantage.

While you may find yourself participating in such a game of wits, it is possible, if not likely, for individuals to demonstrate preferences in how they go about managing this process. The following questionnaire is designed to give you some insight into your own preferences. Complete the questionnaire, then score it to determine what your preferences might be for managing leverage. This will provide you with an unbiased assessment of your preferences before specific techniques are introduced in the chapters that follow.

Negotiation Techniques Questionnaire

For each of the behaviors or techniques listed below, indicate how frequently you use the behavior in your negotiations. Use the scale shown below, where 1 = very infrequently and 7 = very frequently. There are no right or wrong responses, so be as honest and accurate as possible.

| 1 | 2 | 3 | 4 | 5 | 6 | 7 |

Very
Infrequently

Neither
Infrequently
Nor Frequently

Very
Frequently

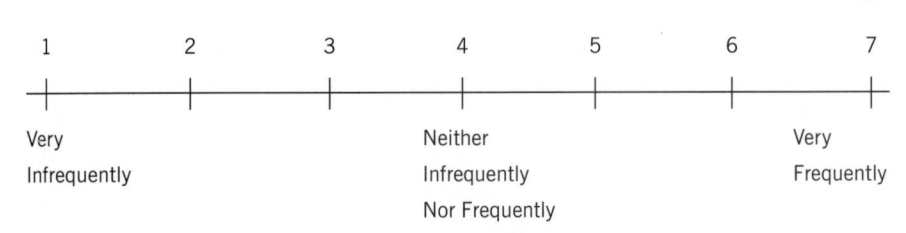

Think about your negotiation experiences overall (personal and professional), as both a buyer and seller of products, services, and ideas. Indicate how frequently you use each behavior by writing a number from 1 to 7 (as shown above) in the space below.

When negotiating, I try to . . .

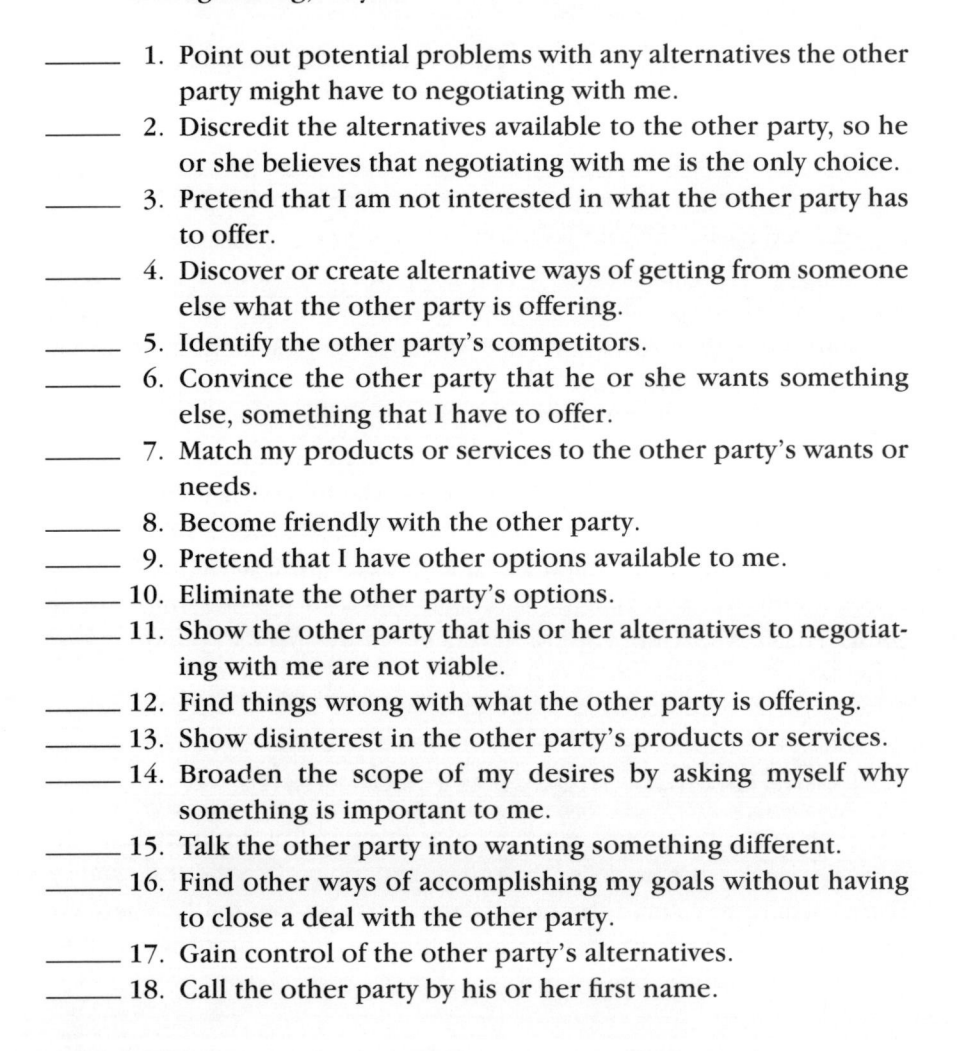

_____ 1. Point out potential problems with any alternatives the other party might have to negotiating with me.
_____ 2. Discredit the alternatives available to the other party, so he or she believes that negotiating with me is the only choice.
_____ 3. Pretend that I am not interested in what the other party has to offer.
_____ 4. Discover or create alternative ways of getting from someone else what the other party is offering.
_____ 5. Identify the other party's competitors.
_____ 6. Convince the other party that he or she wants something else, something that I have to offer.
_____ 7. Match my products or services to the other party's wants or needs.
_____ 8. Become friendly with the other party.
_____ 9. Pretend that I have other options available to me.
_____ 10. Eliminate the other party's options.
_____ 11. Show the other party that his or her alternatives to negotiating with me are not viable.
_____ 12. Find things wrong with what the other party is offering.
_____ 13. Show disinterest in the other party's products or services.
_____ 14. Broaden the scope of my desires by asking myself why something is important to me.
_____ 15. Talk the other party into wanting something different.
_____ 16. Find other ways of accomplishing my goals without having to close a deal with the other party.
_____ 17. Gain control of the other party's alternatives.
_____ 18. Call the other party by his or her first name.

Managing Leverage

_____ 19. Point out to the other party that there are other people with whom I could do business.
_____ 20. Determine what the other party wants or needs, so I can offer it.
_____ 21. Point out to the other party that other alternatives to closing a deal with me are flawed.
_____ 22. Understand why I need what I am asking for.
_____ 23. Point out deficiencies in what the other party is trying to sell me.
_____ 24. Find friends in common with the other party.
_____ 25. Create options or alternatives to negotiating an agreement with the other party.
_____ 26. Pretend I do not need what the other party is offering.
_____ 27. Pretend that I can get the other party's product or service somewhere else.
_____ 28. Shift the other party's perceptions from what he or she wants to something else that I can provide.
_____ 29. Determine the other party's competitors, who can also satisfy my needs.
_____ 30. Find ways to neutralize or eliminate the other party's alternatives through alliances with others.
_____ 31. Point out why any options that the other party says he or she has are inferior to what I have to offer.
_____ 32. Point out reasons why the other party's product or service might not meet my needs.
_____ 33. Understand the reasons behind my desires, and whether or not there are other ways of accomplishing these broader ends.
_____ 34. Pretend that I have more choices or options available to me, with other individuals or companies.
_____ 35. Find out what the other party's wants or needs are.
_____ 36. Work with others to reduce or eliminate the other party's options.

Scoring the Questionnaire

You probably noticed that some of the questions were repetitious. This was done on purpose, to make sure that there was some reliability in measuring your perceived use of a particular technique.

The questionnaire focuses on eleven techniques for managing leverage. These techniques fall into two broad categories of interests—techniques for increasing your leverage, and techniques for decreasing your counterpart's leverage.

To score the questionnaire, you will need to move the numbers you recorded to the scoring sheet shown in Table 7-1. For example, your numbers for questions 7, 20, and 35 concern the technique "Match your products/services to counterpart's wants/needs." Add these three numbers and record the total to the right of those numbers in the Scoring Table under the column labeled Totals-Technique. Do the same for each of the other techniques. Under the column labeled Totals-Focus, add the three numbers in the Technique column. Do the same for all four sets of three numbers. Under the column Totals-Interest, add the two numbers in the Focus column to determine your score (preference) for increasing your leverage. Do the same for the other two numbers in the Focus column to determine your score and preference for decreasing your counterpart's leverage. (Please note, the numbers in parentheses represent the maximum score for each Technique—21, each Focus—63, and each Interest—126.)

These numbers will make more sense to you once each of the techniques has been explained. After this explanation is given, some averages will be provided to better help you evaluate the scoring of the questionnaire.

Table 7-1. Scoring table: techniques for altering leverage.

					Totals	
Interest	Focus	Techniques	Scoring	Technique (21)	Focus (63)	Interest (126)
Increasing Your Leverage	Counterpart's Wants/Needs	Match your products/services to counterpart's wants/needs.	7 + 20 + 35 = ___			
		Alter counterpart's perceived wants/needs.	6 + 15 + 28 = ___			
		Tap affiliation needs.	8 + 18 + 24 = ___			
	Counterpart's Alternatives	Discredit other alternatives.	2 + 11 + 21 = ___			
		Eliminate counterpart's alternatives (e.g., through merger or alliance).	10 + 17 + 30 = ___			
		Combination of these two techniques	1 + 31 + 36 = ___		___	
Decreasing Counterpart's Leverage	Your Wants/Needs	Feign disinterest in counterpart's product/service.	3 + 13 + 26 = ___			
		Identify product/service deficiencies.	12 + 23 + 32 = ___			
		Expand purpose of your pursuit.	14 + 22 + 33 = ___		___	
	Your Alternatives	Identify counterpart's competitors.	5 + 19 + 29 = ___			
		Create viable alternatives.	4 + 16 + 25 = ___			
		Feign other options.	9 + 27 + 34 = ___	___	___	___

8

> Like it? Well, I don't see why I oughtn't like it. Does a boy get a chance to whitewash a fence every day?
>
> —Tom Sawyer

Increasing Your Leverage

As suggested by the scoring of the questionnaire, there are two ways of managing leverage: You can increase your leverage, or you can decrease the other party's leverage. This chapter deals with the former; the next chapter addresses the latter.

Essentially, there are two ways of increasing your leverage—by affecting the other party's wants and needs, or by affecting the alternatives the other party perceives to be available.

The Other Party's Wants and Needs

There are several ways of addressing the other party's wants and needs. You can: Match your products or services to the other party's needs, alter the other party's conception of what he or she wants or needs, or take advantage of the other party's affiliation needs.

Match Your Product or Service to Counterpart's Wants and Needs. In an episode of the television show "Sex and the City," Samantha discovers that she has breast cancer. Unhappy with the assessment and advice of her physician, she decides to get a second opinion. But not just from any doctor. This new doctor has been rated *the* top oncologist by *New York Magazine* for the past four years. Unfortunately, this doctor is booked solid for months. Undeterred, Samantha decides to camp out in the waiting room, hoping for a cancellation. She is not

- 45 -

alone, as a nun with a similar diagnosis has been waiting even longer. The young receptionist is adamant—there are no openings. Samantha drops every name she can think of, but nothing works. Then, during the second day, the receptionist opens a magazine and sees a picture of Samantha with her much younger and famous boyfriend Smith Jerrod (known as the Absolut Hunk), who just happens to be the receptionist's favorite heartthrob. (His picture serves as her computer's screen saver.) Samantha offers to bring him to the waiting room, and suddenly the receptionist is more than willing to schedule an early-morning appointment, which the doctor does not like but will occasionally tolerate. Samantha gets an appointment for the nun as well.

The first way to affect the other party's wants and needs involves matching what you have to offer (your products or services) to the other party's needs. Sometimes you can gain information prior to engaging the other party face-to-face, such as by talking with people familiar with the other party, searching the Internet for reports, analyses, and profiles, and so on. Large companies, for example, target their marketing ads on data collected from multiple sources by companies like Acxiom Corporation, which develops detailed patterns in consumer behavior based on credit-card purchases, warranty registrations, etc.

Samantha might have done the same, by trying to learn more about this particular doctor's office before arriving or from others in the waiting room. Once at the office, Samantha wasted a lot of time dropping names rather than trying to find out what the receptionist valued. In the end she got lucky, but she only succeeded due to that good fortune. Rather than making declarative statements (dropping names), she would have been better off asking questions and observing the receptionist carefully.

Skilled job applicants are good at doing this. Rather than going into an interview with resume in hand, prepared to sell their skills and accomplishments, and braced to answer whatever question might be thrown at them, skilled interviewees are the ones asking the questions: "Tell me what you are looking for in the ideal candidate?" "What will make the person who takes this position successful?" "Where do you see the company going in five years?" Armed with the information, this candidate then can tailor her experiences and skill-set so that she appears to be the perfect fit for the company.

Asking questions, particularly open-ended questions—questions

Increasing Your Leverage 47

that cannot be answered with a single word or short phrase—is a good way of identifying the other party's wants or needs. An open-ended question in effect says "Tell me what's on your mind . . . what is pressing on your mind." If you cannot tell what is on someone's mind from experience or observation (for example, an item they keep examining), you need to ask. And then you need to show how what you have to offer matches those wants and needs.

As suggested by the examples above, open-ended questions can come in the form of a question (for example, "How can I help you today?") or a statement that requests information or elaboration ("Tell me how I can help you" or "Tell me more"). A similar outcome can be achieved through reflective inquiries, in which you parrot back what the party has said. For example, if you are selling furniture and a prospective buyer says to you "We're here to look at sofas," you might respond "So, you are interested in sofas," or just "Sofas?" This is a reflective response that implicitly requests additional information.

An important part of gaining useful information about the other party's wants or needs is exercising the right blend of asking questions and providing information. While offering alternatives and gauging another party's response can yield some information, asking questions generally yields more information. This makes silence an important tool in negotiating. Sometimes silence alone is the best tactic you can employ, and certainly following an open-ended question or inquiry. Silence makes many of us uncomfortable to the point of jumping in and offering valuable information about our wants and needs.

Alter Counterpart's Perceived Wants or Needs. A second way of affecting the other party's perception that you have what he wants is by altering the other party's conception of what it is he wants and needs. This is perhaps easiest when the other party enters the negotiation uncertain about what he wants. Mark Twain's classic tale of Tom Sawyer, who was given the chore of whitewashing the family fence, illustrates this approach. As his childhood friends walk by, Tom creates the perception that there is nothing he would rather be doing on this beautiful day than whitewashing this fence: "Does a boy get a chance to whitewash a fence every day?" It is a rare opportunity that he would not give up or share just for the sake of friendship. And it is the front fence, the one facing the street for everyone to see, not the back fence. As more boys join in, less space remains for everyone else to be added; there are only so many brushes and so much fence. The other boys, having the freedom to do whatever they choose on this summer Saturday, and not altogether clear on how they want to spend it, eventually offer goods in exchange for their turn to work a brush.

A real estate agent, who technically represents the seller, points out a number of features upon first approaching a new property with a prospective buyer—the small front yard (which is easy to care for), good shade from neighboring trees, a slate roof (which is durable). While none of these would necessarily be on the buyer's list of required features, the agent is seeking to alter the prospective buyer's conception of what is important in a house. Likewise, a company looking to buy an electronic security system might be convinced by the sales representative of a security personnel provider that hiring security personnel would be a better alternative, as onsite personnel can respond immediately to any breach in security as well as provide other services (admits, escorts, and so on). And, an automotive parts supplier, seeking to merge with its chief competitor, pitches the idea as an opportunity to create "the world's largest automotive parts distributorship." The proposal even includes an offer to put the competitor's name first in the combined (hyphenated) name of the new company. Even a shoe salesperson, failing to find the color, style, or size of your requested shoe in the back room, will likely bring out shoes of a different color, style, or even size, trying to get you to change your preferences.

As these examples might suggest, affecting the other party's conception of what he or she wants often focuses on the world of possibilities. Advertising agencies do this when they create a "sample" ad campaign for a potential client, a presentation that is at once breathtaking and unaffordable. The presentation sells the agency rather than the campaign, appealing to the client's imagination and ego. Fashion designers do the same when they introduce their new lines of spring fashions, many of which are impractical but captivating. It often helps to know your client or client group to recognize which ideas will capture their imagination. At one point during his quest to bring John Sculley from Pepsi to Apple Computer, company cofounder Steve Jobs asked: "Do you want to spend the rest of your life selling sugared water or do you want a chance to change the world?"

A special case of using this second technique to affect the other party's perception of what she wants or needs is the introduction of future opportunities. Some business negotiators, for example, will allude to the possibility of a long-term relationship, leading to increased sales or purchases. On occasion, this may be part of what a seller wants and hopes for from a buyer. An apartment manager, for example, needs someone to quickly repair gutters that were damaged by a storm, which might lead to a long-term contract to clean the gutters semiannually. On other occasions, such as selling your home to another party because you are retiring to another region of the country, there may be little likelihood of future contact. In that case, an invitation to "stop by and visit the house at any time" may be more fanciful than likely.

The ability to alter what a party really wants, or at least cast light on an issue or feature that did not seem especially important at the outset of the negotiation, is what separates the average salesperson from the great salesperson. The expression "he could sell sand to a man in the desert" captures this capability: A man in the desert would have no use or interest in more sand, but somehow an accomplished salesperson could redirect the man's interests from water or food to believing that what he needs most is more sand.

Tap Affiliation Needs. A third way of affecting the other party's wants and needs is by recognizing that individuals also have social or "affiliation" needs, which represent a potential source of loss or "cost" in a negotiation. Recall that leverage is relationally based; it exists only as long as the relationship exists. If a relationship is important to one party but not so highly valued by the other party, then the relationship can be the basis for exercising leverage. This is most apparent in young children, who learn at some point that telling another child "I will not be your friend if you don't give me what I want" often produces capitulation. (When used on a parent, this ruse is generally taken at face value and defused with a statement like "I'll love you anyway.")

Affiliation needs can be engendered by making the other party feel welcome, important, or part of the team. When the other party makes a mistake or blunder, you say: "Oh, that's happened to me, too." When the other party approaches something in a different way, you respond: "I never thought of it that way before." By listening to the other party's stories or responding with affirmation at critical points, you implicitly communicate that you are more alike than different and, where you are different, that there is something special about the other party.

A friend told me about how she and her husband lost out on a bid for a house, despite making a very attractive offer. It turned out that the couple selling the house had already developed an affinity for the "winning" couple, that was expecting the birth of twins within the next few months. The winning couple had actually enclosed a copy of the mother-to-be's sonogram with their bid.

Many of the advertisements we see on television feature well-known sports figures and other celebrities. These ads are intended to tap our affiliation needs. We want to be like the hero of the last Super Bowl, the star of the hit television series, or the singer whose recording is now topping the charts. We feel as if they are speaking directly to us. If they use it and endorse it, we want it.

Most salespeople tap affiliation needs instinctively. They shake your hand, call you by your first name, tell you funny stories, laugh at your jokes, connect with you on multiple levels. Their friendly, gregarious approach is either part of their personalities, or they have learned through trial-and-error that customers who like them are more inclined to buy their product or service.

Humor can provide an effective means of building social bridges, if it is done properly. Self-deprecating humor, for example, portrays an individual as "human," someone who makes mistakes and who does not see himself as superior to others. In some cases, this is a necessary condition to building a sense of affiliation. Often political figures will do this, as a way of showing that they are "one of the people." Bill Clinton joked about his love of fast foods; George W. Bush made fun of his English syntax. (Humor also implies that the stakes are not that important to you, a potential means of decreasing the other party's leverage, which is discussed in the next chapter.)

Tapping the other party's affiliation need is something that can even be accomplished at the very end of a negotiation. An individual who is selling a desktop computer and agrees to help the other party set it up and learn how to use it (or, alternatively, the individual who throws in some software or a microphone and camera) is likely to gain some affiliation points. That is, you feel some admiration or respect for the individual, which you now don't want to lose. Sometimes what is offered as a type of add-on or sweetener at the end of the negotiation is really of little or no value to the party who is making the offer or gesture. For example, a woman selling her car would have little use for the two snow tires that fit only this particular model. So in throwing the tires in, she is actually getting rid of something with very little value to her. When such an item is initially held out as important, the tactic is referred to as a strawman tactic. That is, an issue or item that is portrayed as having value is later traded for something else of value (in this case, affiliation points).[1]

The Other Party's Alternatives

The other way of increasing your leverage is by focusing on the other party's alternatives. There are two ways to accomplish this. You can discredit the other party's alternatives or eliminate the other party's alternatives.

Discredit Counterpart's Alternatives. If the company seeking a security system mentioned previously is convinced that using security personnel is preferable, and knows of another security firm that provides such personnel, then the security personnel provider can increase its leverage by changing the company's perception of the viability of the other firm. This can be done in a variety of ways, such as indicating that the other firm has been having financial problems and there are rumors that they may go out of business. Who would want to sign a two-year agreement with a company about to go bankrupt?

History is replete with examples of companies, if not entire industries, trying to discredit another company or its product. The inventor Thomas Edison, a proponent of direct current, tried to discredit alternating current as unsafe, going so far as to electrocute an elephant with alternating current. Dairy producers sought to discredit the introduction of alternative spreads, such as margarine. Wendy's ran a memorable commercial for its hamburgers that asked "Where's the beef?" intending to discredit the likes of McDonald's. Cable providers attempt to show the limitations of satellite dishes. Gas companies describe the shortcomings of oil-derived heat. Brick and masonry companies seek to discourage homeowners from building wood houses.

Discrediting occurs in electoral politics as well. In presidential elections, for example, a candidate will paint his or her opponent as too young or too old, as inexperienced, wishy-washy, and so on, as a way of discrediting his or her ability to govern. A candidate will also try to characterize his or her opponent as an extremist, representing the far left or right. By claiming the center of the political spectrum, the candidate hopes to limit the appeal of the other party to the smallest possible portion of the electorate.

Obviously, there is some risk involved in discrediting alternatives. In politics, it is viewed as negative campaigning, which can create a perception of desperation. In business, also, an individual must be careful regarding when and how discrediting alternatives is handled. A business owner who is quick to discredit a competitor may appear to be purely self-interested. There are more subtle ways to accomplish this, which we'll discuss a bit later.

Eliminate Counterpart's Alternatives. The other party's options or alternatives also can literally be eliminated. Companies, for example, often take actions to materially reduce or eliminate the alternatives of their competitors through alliances, coalitions, mergers, and buyouts. Airlines merge in order to link domestic and international routes (which are restricted by air space and airport gates), and lock their competitors out of certain markets. During the 1990s, e-mail and Internet providers were looking to link up with telephone, cable, and broadcast companies, which are limited and regulated in the United States by the Federal Communications Commission, in anticipation of a burgeoning integrated communication/entertainment market. Since there were only a small number of major companies with which to partner, formalizing a partnership would limit the alternatives available to competitors.

In the nineteenth and twentieth centuries, many coalmining companies in the United States required their employees to purchase products at the "company store." This was a general store operated by the mining company, a store in which prices were almost always inflated. Miners even had to purchase the tools of their trade (such as blasting powder) from the company store. To ensure that they did, a mining company would pay employees in its own money (called "scrip"), which could only be used in its store. Needless to say, miners never saw much take-home pay. This practice was a severe form of alternative elimination.

A similar practice, also designed to keep the price of goods artificially high and, in effect, eliminate competition, is price fixing. The major businesses in an industry will sometimes collude to fix the prices of their products or services, as a way of effectively eliminating competition and reducing consumer alternatives. In recent years, the airline industry, toy manufacturers, vitamin makers, and major music companies dealing in compact discs have all been accused of such practices.

Countries are not beyond such actions as well. As early as the sixteenth century, many European nations forbade their colonies in the New World from purchasing finished products from any country other than the mother country. This practice, called mercantilism, involved taking raw materials from the colony for use in manufacture in Europe. Even the ships in which materials were transported were restricted. Thus, a colony became highly dependent on the mother country, and no other competing European country benefited in any way. Spain, for example, followed this practice with many of its colonies in Latin America.

As some of these examples suggest, time can be an important element in negotiations. The longer an e-mail or Internet provider waits to pursue a partnership with a cable provider, the greater the risk that someone else will form an alliance. As the number of viable partners dwindles over time, the leverage of the remaining telephone, cable, and broadcast companies grows. Thus, it might be to the advantage of a cable provider to delay action, particularly if they are expecting a consolidation in the telephone, cable, and broadcast industries (that is, mergers and acquisitions within the industry resulting in fewer telephone, cable, and broadcast companies).

These represent the primary techniques for increasing leverage. There are also techniques for decreasing the other party's leverage. The next chapter discusses these.

Note

1. In a study of 248 managers, Fred Luthans, Richard Hodgetts, and Stuart Rosenkrantz discovered a significant difference between the activities of successful managers and the activities of effective managers (Fred Luthans, et al., *Real Managers*, Cambridge, Mass.: Ballinger, 1988). Successful managers (managers who had been promoted relatively quickly) had engaged in significantly more networking (socializing, politicking) than had effective managers (managers who accomplished high-performance standards through the commitment and hard work of subordinates and associates). The latter relied significantly more on routine information exchange (answering procedural questions, conveying the results of meetings, writing reports/memos/letters, processing mail, financial reporting, and so on) in their daily activities. This finding illustrates the importance of affiliation in organizational politics and advancement.

9

> I would never want to belong to a club that would have me as a member.
>
> —GROUCHO MARX

DECREASING THE OTHER PARTY'S LEVERAGE

Rather than seeking to increase your leverage, you might effect the same result by choosing to decrease leverage of the other party. As with increasing your own leverage, there are two primary ways to decrease the other party's leverage—by focusing on wants and needs and by focusing on alternatives. In this case, however, it is *your* wants/needs and alternatives that are the key.

Your Wants and Needs

There are three techniques that focus on your wants or needs: feigning disinterest in a counterpart's product or service, identifying product/service deficiencies, and expanding the purpose of your endeavor.

Feign Disinterest in Counterpart's Product or Service. Because the other party's leverage increases when your desire for something that he or she possesses increases, the first way to affect your counterpart's leverage is by tempering your desire . . . or at least the perception of it. One way to do this is by feigning disinterest in what the other party has to offer. As buyers, we frequently do this by claiming that we are just window shopping. We pretend that we are not interested in anything in particular, but rather just killing time. If we can point to a friend who is the only reason for our being in the store, or argue that our spouse is somewhere in the mall doing the real buying, it can be all the

– 55 –

more convincing. (In effect, this technique moves the other party from Active to Blind leverage.)

Our ability to pull this off is related to the type and location of the store we are visiting. It is one thing to be walking home with groceries and stop at a yard sale, and it is another thing to pull up at a car dealership on the outskirts of town just as the showroom is opening. The latter suggests that your visit was planned, and that you are hoping to satisfy a specific need by making this special effort to get to the dealership.

The following behaviors are subtle indicators of the intensity of your interest as a buyer:

1. *Your Pace.* The faster you move, in general, and the faster you move toward the object of your intention, the stronger you signal having a need you believe the other party can satisfy.
2. *The Number of Calls or Visits You Make.* When you return to an individual, an organization, or to a particular item within an organization (such as a retail store), it not only signals that you think the other party can satisfy your want or need, but that you have likely checked elsewhere and concluded this is the best of all options.
3. *Your Focus on the Item of Desire.* Looking directly at it, talking about it, trying it on, etc., suggests that you have a serious interest in the item. And if there is any hesitation whatsoever, a savvy salesclerk will tell you just how good the coat (or dress or hat) looks on you.

Feigning disinterest also applies if you are the seller. How badly do you want to sell an item, and how strongly are you communicating that desire? Often, a prospective buyer will ask: "Why are you selling your car (or boat or business)?" They are concerned that there is some problem—a current or future problem—motivating you, a problem that could affect their willingness to buy. For example, if you say that the warranty on the car is about to expire, and this model begins to incur maintenance problems from this point forward, they may lose their desire to buy the car or they may ask you to drop the price. If you say that you are leaving the country tonight for a new job and need to sell all your large possessions, this communicates a strong motivation to sell as well . . . and quickly. Thus, it is usually in the seller's best inter-

Decreasing the Other Party's Leverage

ests to play down the reasons for wanting to sell. Responses may include: "I just feel like a change," "I don't need such a big car (house) anymore," or "I don't need to sell the boat, in fact sometimes I am not sure that I want to sell it." In other words, one can decrease another party's leverage by feigning disinterest in selling as well as in buying.

Identify Product or Service Deficiencies. A second technique for decreasing the other party's leverage by managing your wants or needs involves finding faults or deficiencies with the desired product or service. With the previous technique, your wants or needs have yet to be established. With this technique, your need is apparent. However, you appear unconvinced that the other party's product can satisfy your need.

There are several different ways that your dissatisfaction can be communicated. You can be clear about which feature(s) are deficient, or remain vague about these specifics. And you can communicate this verbally or nonverbally, and implicitly or explicitly.

For example, imagine that your company is in the market for new copy machines, and you are looking to get the best price and delivery date possible for a specific model. Knowing that the particular model of interest does not print in color, you ask about this feature, raising doubts about how well the copy machines meet your company's requirements: "This machine doesn't make color copies, does it?" This is an example of an explicit verbal challenge to a specific feature of the product.

An episode of the television show "60 Minutes" demonstrated how some antique dealers will use the deficiency technique in an explicit way. A representative from the television show went into an antique store with a valuable antique, asking if the dealer was interested in buying the piece. The dealer looked it over, and then pointed out some flaw (craftsmanship, missing part). The dealer would offer a modest sum of money for the piece, yet two days later the piece was displayed prominently in his store window with a price tag of ten times the price the dealer paid for the piece. This technique of finding fault or deficiencies was often repeated when other items were taken to other antique dealers. Needless to say, these dealers did not like being confronted on camera when "60 Minutes" representatives returned to their stores to discover the highly marked-up prices.

It is also possible to make a nonverbal challenge to a specific feature. Consider again the case of the copy machines. In examining a particular machine, you open one of the drawers to the paper bin. The drawer opens stiffly. You open and close it several times in the presence of the salesperson, nonverbally communicating that this feature is less than ideal. By specifying that a feature is deficient, you allow the other party to address your concern. The copy machine salesperson comments that the drawer is stiff because the machine is brand new, and it will loosen up in time. Or that a drop of oil can be added to make the drawer open more easily.

Sometimes a presumed deficiency is not specified, verbally or nonverbally, but the apparent dissatisfaction is communicated nonetheless. For example, years ago a well-known recording executive employed this technique on a yet-to-be discovered rock band. The band had been struggling for some time, and had sequestered itself for the purpose of writing new songs. They played the first of their songs for him, a song that would go on to become an international hit. He loved the song, but never revealed his enthusiasm. Instead, he responded stoically, "Anything else?" They played another and then another song for him, each special in its own way, and each time he asked, "Anything else?" Finally, he conceded that a recording contract could be worked out. One of those songs went on to become a number one hit, and the album ultimately went gold.

Finally, the suggestion of deficiencies can be unspecified and nonverbal. A married couple, for example, is having a conflict because the husband forgot an anniversary. Feeling guilty and wanting to make it up to his wife, he offers to take her out to dinner this evening. She remains silent, however, resulting in his qualifying the proposal: They will go to her favorite restaurant. She remains unmoved by this offer, turning her head. He further apologizes, offering that they can go away for the weekend. Her face softens a bit, but she remains silent until he makes one additional modification. They will stay at the honeymoon suite of the Four Seasons hotel.

As mentioned previously, specifying the deficient feature allows the other party to offer explanations (for example, that the stiff drawer on the copy machine will loosen up over time), which may or may not be what you want. The other party may even make some modest concessions, if the deficiency seems significant. But a vague (unspecified, nonverbal) signal can result in the other party providing even more information and concessions.

Decreasing the Other Party's Leverage

Expand the Purpose of Your Endeavor. The third technique for decreasing the other party's leverage through focusing on your wants or needs is a bit more challenging, particularly if you do indeed desire what the other party is offering. This technique involves exploring the reasons for your desire. Imagine, for example, that you are looking to buy a new automobile. If you have a strong desire to buy a new car and you communicate that desire to the salesperson, you increase the salesperson's leverage. However, by asking yourself why you want that new car, you may realize that what you really need is transportation. Suddenly, other solutions, including other forms of transportation, come to mind. These include leasing a car, buying a used car, using public transportation, carpooling with neighbors, etc. By expanding the original purpose of your endeavor—to buy a new car—you open up a new set of options and reduce the strength of your desire. And by reducing the strength of your desire, you decrease the other party's leverage.

Similarly, imagine an ice cream manufacturer that wants to open a store down by the beach. The pursuit of an affordable option leads to negotiations with two or three real estate agents about leasing properties, and preferably only for the warm summer months. Alternatively, the manufacturer might explore the reasons why it wants to expand, such as to sell more ice cream, and then look at alternative ways of accomplishing this goal (for example, contracting with restaurants near the beach, buying a small van that moves throughout the beach selling ice cream, negotiating ice cream as part of school lunch programs, sponsoring an ice cream eating contest, sponsoring a contest for creating a new ice cream flavor). By raising one's needs or purpose to a higher level, a negotiator can often see other ways of accomplishing his or her ends.

You may have noticed the shift in terminology with the preceding examples. We moved from talking about what you *want* to talking about what you *need*. Needs underlie wants—what you want in a given situation is something that will satisfy your need. Often we feel the need (hunger, for example), then we figure out how to satisfy it, which becomes what we want (a candy bar). We may do this subconsciously. But, in fixing our minds on how to acquire what we want, we frequently lose sight of our underlying need (that is, the reason behind our pursuit). When we get frustrated, we may simply focus harder on the means to an end (a candy bar), rather than remind ourselves of the end itself (which, if revisited, can produce new options, in this case other sources of energy or sugar). And as the Rolling Stones immortalized in their song, "You Can't Always Get What You Want," while you may find that "you can't always get what you *want* . . . if you try sometime / you find / you get what you *need*."

Whether you actually pursue other means is not important. What is important is that you realize that you may be able to accomplish your ends through other means. This will reduce your demand for what the other party is offering, and thereby decrease the other party's leverage. And it can help to communicate this revelation to the other party, as well. Say something like "I'm not sure a business partner is what I really need. What I *need* is an investor . . . or investors. Maybe I should just offer stock in the company."

Before we move on, one final observation on wants versus needs. Wants and needs correspond roughly to positions and interests in negotiation. Negotiators sometimes get stuck on their respective positions (wants), unable to see broader interests (needs) that can lead to creative solutions. Sometimes it takes a third party, such as a mediator, to help them find a win-win outcome. Usually this occurs when the mediator asks some variation of "Why?" regarding their positions.[1]

Jimmy Carter, for example, sought to mediate a dispute between Israel and Egypt in the 1970s over a piece of land called the Sinai, which lies between the two countries. Each country established a position that the land was theirs. By asking "Why?" Carter discovered that the Israelis wanted the land for security purposes, while the Egyptians wanted it for historical purposes. These were their needs or interests. This insight eventually led to a solution whereby the Sinai was demilitarized (which satisfied Israel's security need) and Egypt was allowed to fly its flag over the land (which satisfied Egypt's historical need). For this and other works, Jimmy Carter was eventually awarded the Nobel Peace Prize.

Your Alternatives

You also can decrease your counterpart's leverage by focusing on your alternatives. There are three techniques you can use to accomplish this: identifying your counterpart's competitors, creating viable alternatives, or feigning other options.

Decreasing the Other Party's Leverage

Identify Counterpart's Competitors. Sometimes it is enough just to point out to your counterpart the alternative(s) to not reaching an agreement with him or her. Since most every company has a competitor, identifying a viable option available to you (for example, buying from a competitor, merging with a competitor, going to work for a competitor) will at minimum decrease the other party's Active leverage as well as his or her self-confidence.

For many years, many commercial airlines did this for you. Near the end of a flight, one of the flight attendants would close the trip with the following statement: "We know you have a choice of air carriers, and we want to thank you for flying White-knuckle Airline." This was, in effect, an acknowledgment of competitors. (However, by making this statement, they took some of the punch out of the technique. If you don't believe so, try alluding to such options some time when dealing with an airline. You will likely receive a cold response.)

In the real estate business there are "buyers' markets" and "sellers' markets." A buyer's market, which refers to a market in which there are more sellers than buyers, usually occurs when there is a glut of properties (possibly due to overconstruction) and high interest rates. As a buyer, you have options (other properties) to buying any particular property.

In a seller's market these conditions are reversed, leading to high demand for properties and bidding wars. If you are a seller, you hope for a seller's market: You can tell any prospective buyer that there are one or more other buyers ready to put in bids. In other words, as a seller you have options to sell to any one particular individual.

Generally speaking, the more fierce the competition for buyers, the more effective the technique of identifying your counterpart's competitors. This was the case in the 1990s when long-distance telephone companies were battling for every customer they could get, calling consumers on a regular basis with enticements to switch carriers. You often did not have to mention the competition. They did it for you.

Create Viable Alternatives. The second technique for decreasing the other party's leverage by focusing on alternatives is to actually create other options. Some negotiators have been known to take creative and dramatic steps in this regard. In the 1530s, King Henry VIII of England did not like the treatment he was receiving from the Roman Catholic Church. Henry was married to Catherine of Aragon, but wanted a divorce or annulment, as Catherine had not borne him a male heir. The Pope would not grant it. So Henry, in effect, created his own religion by having himself proclaimed the Supreme Head of the Church of England.

Ronald Reagan had only been President of the United States for little more than six months when he faced a strike by the air traffic controllers. Obviously, this was a strike that could shut down the country. Rather than deal with their demands, he fired all of them, replacing the entire corps (a dramatic means of creating one's own alternative). Major League Baseball owners did the same thing late in the 1999 season when about a third of the umpires resigned in an effort to get the owners to the negotiating table. The owners simply hired replacement umpires. In both cases, viable alternatives were created. Looking to gain some independence from the major recording companies, Frank Sinatra formed his own label Reprise Records. The Beatles did the same, founding Apple Records.

A public utility in Texas—Houston Power & Lighting Company—provides another example of how creative and bold some negotiators can be. The utility was paying what it felt were exorbitant fees to Burlington Northern Santa Fe railroad to transport coal to its generating station. The head of purchasing for the public utility could not get the railroad, which operated the only rail line, to agree to a lower rate. Finally, she got the key decision makers of her company to agree to build their own rail line to connect to tracks owned by Union Pacific railroad, ultimately saving her company millions of dollars every year. And when Union Pacific was late with some deliveries, she switched some shipments back to Burlington Northern Santa Fe. Thus, she decreased the leverage of both parties by creating an alternative.

A similar story can be told about Wal-Mart, which became the world's largest retailer by offering a wide variety of goods at very low prices. Wal-Mart encouraged and supported the development of manufacturing in China, where the labor costs are a fraction of those found in the United States. At the point where multiple product manufacturers had been created, Wal-Mart would pit manufacturers against one another through reverse auctions. That is, Wal-Mart buyers would offer an initial low price for a manufactured product, and then ask Chinese manufacturers to bid the price still lower. The more manufacturers Wal-Mart helped to establish, the more competition was created to bid down the price.

Decreasing the Other Party's Leverage

Organizations themselves sometimes can serve as alternatives, through a process called tapered integration. Tapered integration involves a company developing in-house capabilities for supplying some of its inputs or consuming some of its outputs. As a consequence, the company creates alternatives to outside sellers and buyers. One variation of this occurs within franchise industries, where the franchiser maintains some company-owned stores. McDonald's and Holiday Inn, for example, retain a small number of their units to gain information directly about franchise operations, to lead their franchisees by example, and to provide an option (absorbing the unit back into the company) if a franchisee does not meet company expectations.

Time can play a role in the development of alternatives. Skilled negotiators sometimes will hold another party in abeyance while they pursue or create other alternatives. For example, a company seeking a foreign distributor for its products might ask the distributor to provide additional information (company history, sales projections, etc.) while it seeks to identify other potential distributors, or to establish its own distributorships. If an individual is in no hurry, then the creation of alternatives (competition for goods, services) can actually be sequential rather than simultaneous.

It is customary among academics to seek a job offer from another college or university before going up for promotion or tenure at their school. This shows that they are valued in the marketplace and have options. Without such an alternative, a good friend went up for promotion at a university that valued quantity of publications in a range of areas rather than quality in a specialized area, which he had. Consequently, he failed to get the necessary political support from his dean to secure promotion, as he had no apparent alternatives. (He immediately found another school that was eager to hire him at the higher rank, but it meant leaving the town to which his family had grown very attached.)

Feign Other Options. Because leverage is based on perceptions, a negotiator might also try to feign alternatives. As discussed previously, this is less convincing when you are the one approaching the other party and claiming there is a better alternative elsewhere. If the alternative truly is superior, then why are you not pursuing it? Negotiators also can be less direct in creating the perception of alternatives. For example, going to a business meeting in casual attire suggests a you-need-me-more-than-I-need-you attitude, which could be due to the availability of alternatives.

The implication of alternatives is often enacted by expensive restaurants, when you arrive without a reservation. The restaurant may be empty, but the maitre d' nevertheless asks if you have a reservation, checks the reservation list, and hems and haws before finding a table for you. The implication is that the restaurant has options (that is, other patrons competing to eat there). This works best, of course, if you are not a regular diner at the restaurant. A similar scene is occasionally played out in a television comedy or theatrical play, where a sympathetic protagonist who has no social life is asked on a date and pretends to check his or her appointment book for an open day or time. The protagonist is feigning alternatives, as the appointment book is empty (if it is an appointment book at all).

When there really are no alternatives, however, it takes a skilled individual to create and maintain the bluff. In general, bluffing works best when the bluffing party has the right demeanor (normal speech rate, voice pitch, body movements), the bluff appears consistent with prior statements, the bluff comes near the end of the negotiation, and the other party has limited access to contradicting information. The risk is that, if caught, the other party will never believe the bluffing party again, even when he or she is being honest. Perhaps the only thing worse than being caught in a lie or bluff is having the other party convinced you are bluffing when you are not.

Self-Assessment

You should now have a better sense of the different ways of changing leverage, including specific techniques within the two broader categories of increasing your leverage and decreasing your counterpart's leverage. Go back and take a look at the questionnaire you scored (Table 7-1). Which of the eleven techniques received the most points? The second most points? The least points? What do you see as the advantages and disadvantages of your preferences?

More on this later. But first, let's focus a bit on recognizing the different techniques employed in negotiation scenarios. As important as it is to understand your own style, it is equally important to understand the preferences and techniques of others. In a live negotiation, emotions can blunt our ability to analyze a situation clearly and rapidly.

So we begin with several case scenarios, to help you know what to look for.

Note

1. A mediator, who happened to be a psychologist, suggested an alternative query to asking "Why?" When one of the disputants would become focused on his or her position, the psychologist/mediator would ask: "And what will that do for you?" It was another way of refocusing the disputant on needs or interests.

10

> Power is not revealed by striking hard or often, but by striking true.
>
> —Honoré de Balzac

Checking Your Progress: Altering Leverage

Now that you're familiar with the two primary approaches to changing leverage—increasing your leverage or decreasing the other party's leverage—and the techniques associated with each approach, let's see how good you are at identifying what to do in some challenging situations. You will find below four scenarios, each taken in part from a real-life experience. Read each scenario, and then write your response to the questions at the end of each scenario regarding who has the leverage and how it might be changed. Keep in mind for the first of these questions that leverage is based on perceptions, so we are making our best guess as to how the parties perceive one another.

An analysis follows each scenario. But don't jump ahead to the analysis too quickly. Give each scenario your best effort first.

Scenario A

You are traveling in a foreign country, a country that you have visited many times. You have some knowledge of the language spoken, although you are not fluent. You are about halfway into your ten-day visit, traveling alone by rented car to a golf course on the outskirts of the city. You have been to this golf course a couple of times before, and you know that sometimes there are police waiting for speeding motorists, so you are driving carefully. As you approach the speed trap, two policemen standing alongside a city police vehicle motion you to pull over. You have been very careful to observe the speed limit, and cannot understand what the problem might be. One of the policemen comes over to your car and asks to see your driver's license, which you provide. He also asks to see some other documents, including car registration and insurance. You tell him this is a rental car, showing him your rental agreement. He takes the document to the other officer, then comes back and says that you do not have proper insurance so you will have to go to the police station. You ask why, but do not completely understand his response. You rented the car with your credit card, which is supposed to provide insurance. You tell him this. He goes back to the other policeman to discuss your claim, but returns to tell you there is no indication of insurance on the rental agreement.

1. Who has leverage in this situation? _____
2. How can you increase your leverage or decrease the other party's leverage? _____
_____
_____

Analysis: Leverage is determined by the perceived costs incurred by one or both parties in a negotiation. The more it costs the other party not to have an agreement with you, the more leverage you have. With the information given in this scenario, it would appear that the police have some leverage. They have the power to detain you at least, and make life much more difficult should you resist and do something foolish (like attempt to drive off). The fact that you are driving to a golf course for recreational purposes, rather than something more pressing such as your daughter's wedding, means that the costs are likely not as great as they could be in this case, although we don't know for sure, as you may be meeting an important client at the golf course. And, in fact, if you are simply off by yourself to kill some time at a club you've visited before, you might actually welcome a change of pace and not mind to go to the police station out of curiosity.

There are probably several different ways to change the leverage in this situation. If, indeed, you would be more interested in seeing how the police-judicial system works than in playing golf, you might decrease your counterpart's leverage by suggesting that this could be a welcomed adventure for you. This is an example of focusing on your wants or needs, and changing those desires by expanding the purpose of your activity.

The friend who told me this story employed the following approach. Recognizing that this was just a shakedown, designed to get him to pay a sum of money not to be hassled, he pretended that he did not understand the laws of the land. Further, he said that he would need to call a friend, a well-known lawyer who was a regular guest on one of the local television stations that offered a short public-service segment on consumer rights. He said this with some desperation in his voice, suggesting that he had no choice given his limited knowledge of the law and the language. And he said this with reasonable certainty that he had not broken any laws.

Suddenly there were costs for the police in not reaching an agreement. Not only might they have lost their ability to make some additional money through this scheme by having to take him in, but the widespread attention that his lawyer-friend could have brought to this practice might have shut them down altogether and affected any and all of the other police officers doing the same. Thus, these police would have had the wrath of the entire department upon them.

This is an example of two different techniques at play. First, it is an example of decreasing your counterpart's leverage by focusing on your alternatives. By suggesting that he might need to contact his lawyer-friend, the motorist was identifying his counterpart's competitors in interpreting the law. Because the lawyer-friend had a television audience and could potentially create serious problems for the police department, this approach also falls into the category of increasing your leverage by focusing on your counterpart's wants or needs. More specifically, he was altering his counterpart's perceived wants or needs. Rather than wanting to fleece him for some pocket bills before the next unsuspecting motorist came by, they now wanted to keep him from blowing the whistle on this operation altogether.

You may have thought of some other approaches to changing the leverage in this scenario. That's great. In fact, the more ideas you can come up with, the better the likely outcome for you in a real negotiation. Given the ideas just shared, see how many ideas you can come up with for Scenario E, which follows.

Scenario B

Up until last year, you were working for a small marketing firm in Europe. However, the firm had a change in leadership the year before, and you became disenchanted with the pace and direction of the firm. You decided to transition to the nonprofit sector, where marketing has only recently become appreciated. As part of the severance, you were allowed to continue with the marketing firm's group health insurance for one year. Near the end of that year, you began having problems with your sinuses. This was causing headaches and toothaches. By the time you discovered in November that there was some type of cyst in your sinus cavity, your health insurance was about to run out (end of November). Your specialist could do the surgery in early December, but this creates a problem. The new insurance coverage for which you signed up beginning December 1st has a clause that prohibits claims for the first six months of activation. This is to prevent people from signing up for insurance just before a major operation. Your operation will only require one day of hospitalization, but this would still be very expensive if you had to pay for it out-of-pocket. You are not sure, however, that you can wait six months for the surgery (although one doctor you saw believes this is not unreasonable if you take certain precautions in the interim). Your new insurance policy is four times as expensive as your former group health plan, but you made a three-month payment nonetheless. On December 15 you receive a bill from your former group health plan for another month. You do not understand. You thought that plan ended in November. You contact them, and their representative says that you have one more month of coverage. If you had known this, you could have had the surgery under your old plan. You are confused and angry. You contact the insurance agent who sold you the new policy, as she was supposed to have researched all this.

1. Who has leverage in this situation? _____
2. How can you increase your leverage, or decrease the other party's leverage? _____

Analysis: This scenario has several players in it: you, your old health care provider, your new health provider, and the insurance

Checking Your Progress: Altering Leverage

agent who sold you the new policy. For simplicity's sake, let's focus on you and the agent. It would seem that the costs to you of not having an agreement are substantial. This includes not only out-of-pocket expenses (although you have already paid three months of insurance premiums to the new provider) but also the potential health risks and discomfort of waiting to have an operation. What are the likely costs to the agent in this case? If the agent works for a firm, you could report her to the appropriate supervisor. You could also report this matter to a licensing bureau. These costs could translate into loss of business if not a loss of license. So there are some potential costs for the agent, as well.

These latter costs suggest some ways of increasing your leverage. If the agent is young and just getting established in the field, she may not want to risk sanctions or even understand what can be done to counter such an action from you. By recognizing how important this job is to the agent's career aspirations, you can address her wants or needs by urging that some compensation take place. The agent is in a better position to get one or both of the providers to make an exception in your case. Even if the agent is relatively new to the business, she has the ability to move clients toward one provider or another, and the providers know this. And if the agent has an established relationship with select individuals at one or both providers, she can use these to her advantage. In other words, the agent has more leverage with the providers than you would have. (We'll say more about multiparty negotiations later in the book.)

You also can tap affiliation needs with your agent. If you developed a good relationship with the agent from the beginning, it will be harder for her to simply turn your concerns aside. And if you have relationships with other members of her organization, or with other clients, these can work to your advantage as well.

The agent may think that delay or inaction will eventually wear you down. By seeking to discredit or eliminate these alternatives, you increase the costs to her of not taking action on your behalf and, in the process, increase your leverage. There are some ways to do this that are more effective than others. For example, you might want to take the lead and do most of the talking: "Ann, you have been a good agent for me in the past, and I know you are concerned about my welfare. I know you want to do what is right in this case, and act swiftly to make sure that I can have this operation. Any delay could risk my health."

Thus, you paint the alternatives of not taking action or delaying action as inappropriate or unprofessional, without saying so in those exact words.

You can also look for ways of decreasing your counterpart's leverage by decreasing the costs to you of not having an agreement. One approach is to ask yourself why you are pursuing this. The answers might include the need for an operation as well as the money to pay for the operation. Are there ways of delaying the operation for six months, as suggested in the case? You will ultimately need the new insurance, so you are only losing one month of premiums.

Let's try another scenario, this one involving the purchase of a business.

Scenario C

A fairly well-known businessman who owns a printing company in a metropolitan area is interested in selling this business. It is just one of several businesses that he owns. It appears that he may be short of cash, and this company represents a different industry than his other holdings. You have met this man on several occasions, and he contacts you about buying the company. You are potentially interested in purchasing it, and agree to meet with him. The meeting is set for two weeks hence, and you attend the meeting with an associate. During the meeting, you get some sense of what is involved. You agree to meet again in two days to discuss details, including price. You have set a particular price that you are willing to pay, and following some discussions at this next meeting you learn that the asking price is under your expectations. Delighted with this, you agree in principle to buy the printing company. You shake hands. About a week later you notice an ad in a business journal for this company, for a higher price than you agreed to. You try to contact this businessman, but are told that he has decided to put the company back on the market. Apparently, he used you as a sounding board for developing his asking price.

1. Who has leverage in this situation? _____
2. How can you increase your leverage, or decrease the other party's leverage? _____
_____

Checking Your Progress: Altering Leverage

Analysis: The first question that this scenario probably raises in your mind is whether or not a handshake is binding. If it is, then you have the law on your side, which can exert considerable leverage. As a general rule, a handshake is not considered binding, at least in most countries around the world, including the United States. However, that does not mean that it has no significance. If, on the basis of this gentleman's agreement, you were to take out a loan or incur other expenses in anticipation of a signed agreement and transfer of ownership, the courts might award you some damages based on the principle of detrimental reliance, at least in the United States. That is, if you took reasonable actions based on an implicit agreement, incurring certain expenses, the courts might require the other party to reimburse you. These actions and expenses would have to have occurred between the time of the handshake and the discovery that the other party had reneged on the implicit agreement. Therefore, you might have some leverage in this situation, but only to regain lost expenses. The owner of the printing company would appear to have more leverage, at least at the outset.

The principle of detrimental reliance suggests a preventive albeit somewhat risky tactic for you to gain leverage in this situation. The sooner you act following the implicit agreement (handshake) and the more expenses you incur, the more leverage you have if the other party double-crosses you; the more expenses you incur, the more the courts are likely to make the printing company owner pay. However, this represents a substantial risk. Judicial verdicts are not always predictable, yet they are often time consuming and costly. Given that your legal case against the printing company owner is limited, what other options are available to you for changing the leverage in this situation?

Let's focus first on decreasing the other party's leverage. This involves decreasing the costs of not having an agreement with this individual, when you thought you already had one. At this point, there are three primary costs involved: (1) the time that you already invested in reaching the agreement on which you shook hands, (2) the loss of potential profitability from the printing company you thought you had bought, and (3) the damage to your ego, esteem, and reputation from having been tricked by this businessman into giving him your time and professional opinion.

The first of these is a sunk cost, and a marginal one at that. To invest more time and effort for the purpose of recovering lost time and effort makes little sense. Unless, of course, you see the time invested as a warning and lesson in what could happen with unscrupulous businesspeople. By expanding the purpose of your pursuit, you may realize that you want to own a business, but not necessarily a printing company, and you want a business partner who is a trusted friend. Because this might just be the tip of the iceberg in dealing with this particular businessman, you might be better off not having an agreement. Someone who would renege on a handshake might just as easily surprise you in other, more damaging ways (for example, cooked books, hidden debt, unrevealed liens). Or you may realize that you do not necessarily want to own another business, but that you are looking to invest the profits you made through another venture. There may be other ways of investing, such as by purchasing sufficient stocks to have a substantial if not controlling interest in a company.

The possibility of other surprises from the printing company owner raises questions about the second cost—the loss of potential profitability from purchase of the printing company. If, indeed, there are two sets of books or hidden debts, the profitability of the business may be more illusion than reality. By finding alternatives, you decrease your counterpart's leverage by decreasing your costs of not doing business with him. This could be accomplished by finding another printing company to buy or, as suggested above, identifying and pursuing a completely different investment option. Many times all that is necessary is to create the impression that you have alternatives.

The third cost—damage to your ego, esteem, and reputation—is difficult to assess and is determined to some extent by who finds out about this failed transaction. It is reminiscent of an episode of Donald Trump's reality television show "The Apprentice," in which two teams were pitted against each other in renovating and renting an apartment. The project leaders for the two teams had to choose between two apartments to renovate. One of the project leaders, Katrina, had worked in the real estate business, and the other project leader, Troy, had not. How would they decide who got which property to renovate? After they had toured the properties, Katrina suggested that each write down on a piece of paper which apartment they would prefer to renovate, then exchange papers. She wrote down the unit that she believed would have the best chance of winning the contest for her team. Troy did not know the industry, and he wished that he had Katrina's experience to know what factors to consider in selecting a property. So he

Checking Your Progress: Altering Leverage

wrote down "I want exactly what you want" on his slip of paper. In exchanging their papers, Troy learned which apartment Katrina felt had the greatest potential, while Katrina was angry that she had been duped and that Troy had acted unprofessionally. Not able to negotiate an agreement, a coin flip determined who had first choice of properties. Troy won and chose Katrina's preferred property. Ultimately, Troy's team won the contest, and Katrina took her anger to the boardroom in trying to discredit Troy.

If the owner of the printing company is inclined to gloat over tricking you into revealing the market value of the business, you can always feign disinterest in the business and pretend that it is no big deal that you were tricked. You can even point out deficiencies in the business and the contract that you were planning to sign. These techniques focus on your wants or needs. In addition, you can talk about another printing company in which you are interested. This focuses on your alternatives. Most of these techniques represent defensive strategies designed to minimize the perceived embarrassment and damage. However, they could lure the printing company owner back to the negotiation table, particularly if he discovers no other parties expressing interest in his business.

What about increasing your leverage? That is, what about increasing the costs to the other party of not having an agreement with you? First, let's focus on the printing company owner's wants or needs. There are several things you can do in this regard. If you believe that the owner's reputation is of some value to him, you might talk about a professional association to which you belong, implying that you could do considerable damage to his reputation by sharing this story with key association members. This has to be done tactfully, of course. You could begin by laughing off the incident, shaking hands, pretending that nothing is amiss. Then recount a similar incident that happened to a friend at the professional association, who told you and others about the experience. If you can link your story to someone that the printing company owner knows in the association, all the better.

You might recognize through conversations with the owner an essential reason why the printing company has failed to perform up to expectations, and introduce yourself or your company as the answer to that need. If the printing company has failed to adequately market its unique services to the public, and marketing is your particular expertise (and what drew the printing company owner to you in the first place), you could show how your special talents are just what the owner needs.

You also can alter the owner's perceived wants or needs. For example, you might talk about a friend and business associate from California who is planning to open several business centers in your region. Each will offer a wide variety of business services, including printing. You could mention that your friend will be looking for a company to provide printing services.

Another way to increase your leverage is by focusing on the owner's alternatives. This involves either discrediting or eliminating his alternatives. If, for example, you were to make public that you had an agreement with him, and that that agreement might supersede any other deal that he made with another party, it could dissuade potential buyers. After all, who would want to invest their time and money in purchasing a printing company, only to have the contract voided by a court ruling that the company had already been sold to you?

You could also seek to dissuade other buyers by sharing your experience with this businessman. This could be done publicly (for example, a court case) or privately (such as through various business associations or networks to which you belong). These approaches, unfortunately, communicate something about you as well as the unscrupulous printing company owner, and you must carefully consider this before taking action.

Here is one final scenario, this involving a situation that many travelers have experienced in one form or another.

Scenario D

You are traveling overseas by plane to make a series of business presentations. You will be gone for three weeks. When you arrive at the airport, you discover that the bag you checked hasn't arrived. You go to the missing baggage counter, explaining the problem. They tell you that your bag missed your connecting flight, and it will be put on the next plane and arrive the following day. Fortunately, your presentation materials are in your briefcase, which you carried on the plane. However, except for a few brochures, which should carry you through tomorrow's initial presentation, the bulk of your brochures were in the bag. In addition, the bag contains your suit and other clothes. The

Checking Your Progress: Altering Leverage

missing baggage attendant offers you $35 to cover expenses until the bag arrives tomorrow, claiming that this is standard procedure.

1. Who has leverage in this situation? _____
2. How can you increase your leverage, or decrease the other party's leverage? _____
_____
_____

Analysis: At first blush, the costs to you seem very real and substantial. There are two items that you are missing—brochures and your clothes (your suit in particular)—neither of which the airline can provide immediately: At least they cannot produce those brochures and your particular suit at this moment, and you need these to make a professional presentation tomorrow. You may be able to replace the suit, but replacing the brochures is more difficult. In terms of the suit, the issue is money; replacing the brochures may take more than money. How badly do you want the suit, and what alternatives are available? This, recall, determines leverage. How badly do you need the brochures, and what alternatives are available? The bottom line is that the airline appears to have some leverage over you because of your perceived costs.

What leverage do you have over them? That is, what are the costs to the airline representative, his or her supervisor, the people responsible for forwarding your bag the next day, and the airline generally of not having an agreement with you? This may appear to be less clear, given the information offered in the case. Without question, the airline has lost more bags than you have over the years. So they are probably more familiar with the protocol, including how to respond to any threats or emotion you might throw at them. The experience and personality of the particular airline representatives that you will deal with in this case, however, might moderate familiarity and demeanor. In the long run, there may be costs that the airline can incur if you are not satisfied with their service. You could stop flying with them, get your company president to contact their president and threaten to switch airlines, file a claim with the Better Business Bureau, try to create bad publicity for the airline. The airline representative can probably see immediately if you are a preferred customer (gold, silver, or platinum card status, for example). But the representative will probably not be aware of any other costs you might inflict. Overall, it appears that the airline has more leverage than you have.

Now, let's talk about some "what ifs." If the airline could ensure that your items will arrive on the next plane, and an early plane, perhaps some of your costs and concerns would abate. If necessary, you can probably buy a suit or at least a sport coat yet today. And you might be able to get your firm to ship you some more brochures overnight, if the few brochures that you have are not sufficient and if you cannot get by on the promise of sending a brochure to a prospective client later in the week. All of this is to suggest that there are two potential costs for you—the cost of replacing these items and the potential cost of losing a client because you look unprofessional or ill prepared.

As this discussion suggests, the costs to you of not having an agreement are not absolute. That is, the costs depend on your ability to replace certain items in order to make a successful presentation. If you can find a way to pull off the presentation, you may not need the airline's support, at least in the short run. Your goal is to make a successful presentation. There are other ways to accomplish this goal, as suggested above, besides getting the airline to assign a single individual to locate and personally escort your bag to your hotel room. In fact, you might see if you can reschedule tomorrow's meeting to later in the day or to the following day. This would allow more time for your bag to arrive, and make the costs to you less prohibitive.

Being able to see the larger purpose is a technique for decreasing the other party's leverage by focusing on your wants or needs (Table 7-1). The technique of "Expanding the purpose of your pursuit" comes about by asking some variation of the question "Why?" Why do you need those brochures and that suit? The answer is to be able to make a good presentation to a client. What other ways exist to make a good presentation? You can find a substitute for the brochures, get another suit, see if another person can do the presentation, or reschedule the presentation, among other ideas. By moving from your wants (the brochures and the suit) to your needs (to make a good presentation), a whole new set of options becomes available that likely would not have occurred to you otherwise.

You might also try a number of other techniques to alter leverage. For example, you might decide to create a fuss, holding up other customers, until you get the service and satisfaction you desire. This is a way of limiting your counterpart's alternative of simply turning to the

Checking Your Progress: Altering Leverage

next passenger. Or, you could try to tap the affiliation needs of the airline representative. Chances are, most people in your position would rant and rave. Taking a completely different approach—calmly developing a rapport so that you are on a first-name basis—may work better. You could ask another airline, which has an earlier schedule, to transport your bag. This effectively creates viable alternatives, decreasing the airline's leverage. It also says, implicitly, that you may be changing your preferred carrier.

What makes this case more complex is the number of parties involved. There is the airline representative you are dealing with directly, his or her boss, the people who located your bag, the individuals who set airline policy, and the customer service people with the airline who likely handle claim adjustments. Each has some leverage with the other, which can create complications or opportunities for you. We will talk more about multiparty negotiations in a later chapter.

You may have thought of some additional ways of changing leverage. Generally, the more ways you can think up, the better off you are in a negotiation.

> Polite conversation is rarely either.
> —Fran Lebowitz

11

The Dance of Leverage

Individuals can have strong preferences for how they go about altering leverage—a style, if you will. Many negotiators, however, will change their approach depending on the situation. Their approach is apparent in their manner of engagement and choice of words.

It is interesting to imagine what might happen when parties with similar or different approaches to altering leverage face one another. Imagine a negotiation, for example, in which both parties are trying to decrease the other's leverage. The following dialogue suggests how this might unfold in a retail setting.

> A customer enters an appliance store to buy a washing machine and begins to walk around.
>
> SALESMAN: *Can I help you, sir?*
>
> CUSTOMER (without giving eye contact): *No, that's okay. I'm just looking.* [Feigning disinterest]
>
> SALESMAN: *Excuse me, please.* (walks off in the direction of another customer) [Creating viable alternatives]
>
> CUSTOMER (after some time browsing, finally makes his way to the area of the washing machines, where the salesman also happens to be): *Hmm.*
>
> SALESMAN: *Are you interested in washing machines?*
>
> CUSTOMER: *Oh, I'm not sure. This machine does not have a time-delay feature, allowing you to program the start and stop times.* [Feigning disinterest, Identifying product deficiencies]

SALESMAN: *No, this model does not.*

CUSTOMER: *Carson Appliance carries Kenmore, which has that feature.* **[Feigning other options]**

SALESMAN: *Yes, but you will pay twice as much for one of their washers. Excuse me.* (leaving to attend to another customer) **[Creating viable alternatives or Feigning other options]**

It reads a bit like a dance in which neither party wants to be on the dance floor, doesn't it?

Now let's look at the same encounter, only in this case the customer is still trying to decrease the salesman's leverage but the salesman is trying to increase his leverage.

SALESMAN: *Can I help you, sir?*

CUSTOMER (without giving eye contact): *No, that's okay. I'm just looking.* **[Feigning disinterest]**

SALESMAN: *If you are looking for a best buy, this is the one. Consumer Reports rated it one of the top three models . . . and it is very energy efficient.* **[Match your products to counterpart's needs]**

CUSTOMER (after some time gazing around): *Hmm.*

SALESMAN: *My name is John, by the way. I think I've seen you at some soccer matches in the neighborhood.* **[Setting up to Tap affiliation needs]**

CUSTOMER: *Yes, my daughter plays on Saturdays. I'm Carl Fisher. This machine does not have a time-delay feature, allowing you to program the start and stop times.* **[Identifying product deficiencies]**

SALESMAN: *My daughter does too. She really enjoys it. Does your daughter go to Winthrop Elementary as well, Carl?* **[Setting up to Tap affiliation needs]**

CUSTOMER: *No.*

SALESMAN: *You have a good eye for details, Carl. Are you concerned about energy efficiency? Because this machine uses 20 percent less energy and 40 percent less water. And it has touchpad controls, Carl.* **[Altering counterpart's perceived wants/needs]**

CUSTOMER: *Carson Appliance carries Kenmore, which is programmable.* **[Feigning other options]**

SALESMAN: *Yes, but the models they carry do not have touchpad controls . . . or a hand-wash cycle for your daughter's clothes.* **[Discredit other alternatives]**

What if the roles were reversed, with the customer trying to increase his leverage while the salesman is trying to decrease the customer's leverage? Here is how it might play out.

The Dance of Leverage

SALESMAN: *Can I help you, sir?*

CUSTOMER: *I hope so. Hi, I am Carl Fisher. I understand you have a lot of washing machines in stock.* [**Setting up to Tap affiliation needs, Match your products/services—money—to counterpart's needs**]

SALESMAN: *Excuse me, please.* (walks off in the direction of another customer) [**Creating viable alternatives**]

CUSTOMER (after salesman returns to the area of the washing machines): *Excuse me. Can you help me?*

SALESMAN: *Yes. Sorry, we are so busy these days. Are you interested in washing machines?* [**Identify counterpart's competitors**]

CUSTOMER: *You are John Arnold, aren't you? I think I have seen you at soccer matches on Saturdays. My daughter plays. Do you have a son or daughter who plays as well?* [**Setting up to Tap affiliation needs**]

SALESMAN: *Yes, I have a daughter who plays. Excuse me one moment* (attending to another customer with a question). [**Creating viable alternatives**]

CUSTOMER: *John, could you help me out here? My wife told me to bring back a washing machine. If I don't buy something today, I am going to be in trouble.* [**Matching your products/services—quick purchase—to counterpart's wants/needs**]

SALESMAN: *You and about a half-dozen other people in the store.* [**Identify counterpart's competitors**]

You may have encountered a situation similar to this at one time or another. There was a time when a handful of computer stores were so popular that the sales staff didn't seem to have time to answer questions about new technologies; they went straight to: "Do you want to buy one?" However, you might well find the same atmosphere in any popular, well-established retail store holding its annual store-wide sale, or in a department store the day after Thanksgiving (which kicks off the holiday shopping season in the United States).

Finally, how might this encounter unfold if both parties are attempting to increase their leverage? Consider the following dialogue.

SALESMAN: *Can I help you, sir?*

CUSTOMER: *I hope so. Hi, I am Carl Fisher. I understand you have a lot of washing machines in stock.* [**Setting up to Tap affiliation needs, Match your products/services—money—to counterpart's needs**]

SALESMAN: *Carl, nice to meet you. My name is John. I think I've seen you at some soccer matches in the neighborhood.* [**Setting up to Tap affiliation needs**]

CUSTOMER: *Yes, my daughter plays on Saturdays.* [**Setting up to Tap affiliation needs**]

SALESMAN: *My daughter does too. She really enjoys it. Does your daughter go to Winthrop Elementary as well, Carl?* [**Setting up to Tap affiliation needs**]

CUSTOMER: *No, she doesn't. Say, John, you seem to have a lot of machines in stock, and I am interested in buying. Let's see if we can make a deal.* [**Match your products/services—money—to counterpart's needs—a sale**]

SALESMAN: *If you are looking for a best buy, Carl, this is the one. Consumer Reports rated it one of the top three models . . . and it is very energy efficient.* [**Match your products to counterpart's needs**]

CUSTOMER: *Yes, but it is very expensive, no? At this price, you are going to have trouble selling them, aren't you, John? Have you had many buyers for this particular machine?* [**Discredit other alternatives—buyers**]

SALESMAN: *Actually, yes Carl, because this machine uses 20 percent less energy and 40 percent less water. And it has touchpad controls, Carl.* [**Altering counterpart's perceived wants and needs**]

CUSTOMER: *Is the price cash or credit? I can pay cash if the price is right, John.* [**Altering counterpart's perceived wants and needs**]

SALESMAN: *I could possibly go lower if you paid cash, Carl. And if you picked it up yourself (rather than having us deliver the machine), I can drop the price another $50.* [**Match your products to counterpart's needs**]

You probably noticed that these four sets of dialogue have very different feels to them. The last of the four seems supportive and cooperative compared to most if not all of the others.

When the buying situation was first introduced—a customer entering an appliance store to purchase a washing machine—it might have appeared that the sales staff would have all the leverage. The customer was the party initiating contact and also the one traveling to conduct business, both indicators of the other party's presumed advantage. However, notice how wait times, eye contact, interruptions, response time, and persistence (or lack thereof) were used to signal other sources of leverage, real or fictitious, during the encounters. Leverage really is a perceptual and dynamic social process.

The leveraging behavior of an individual can be determined by his or her personality, or it might be dictated by the situation. As suggested at the end of the third dialogue, a retail store's annual sale might create a situation where the customers dramatically outnumber the sales personnel and, perhaps, even product availability.

Also, keep in mind that the four dialogues represent more or less

The Dance of Leverage

pure approaches by the two parties. In reality, an individual might employ a mix of techniques, sometimes focusing on increasing one's own leverage and other times using techniques intended to decrease the other party's leverage.

Recognizing your own tendencies as well as the techniques and style of another party is important. Being able to manage this process (changing levers, if you will) is another matter. With some practice, you should be able to develop dexterity in using each of the approaches and most if not all of the techniques. Are you ready to try?

12

> A ship in harbor is safe—but that is not what ships are for.
>
> —John A. Shedd

Reality Test

It's time to put some of these ideas into action, and to begin to develop some new skills.

Most everyone has a long-distance telephone service provider—AT&T, MCI, Sprint, etc. (If you don't, for the purpose of this exercise, explore acquiring one.) Each provider generally has a number of different plans, and offers enticements to get you to switch to their service. There is a good chance that you can get a better deal than your current provider is offering, if you negotiate well. You may even get your current provider to sweeten your current plan in order to keep you as a customer.

Before contacting any provider, including your current provider, let's do a leverage audit. That is, let's try to determine how much it will cost each party not to have an agreement with the other party. Keep in mind that these are perceived costs, which vary by individual. Let's say one of your wants/needs is inexpensive weekend calls to Germany. If this is very important to you, you will assign the strength of this want/need a six or seven. What kind of service to Germany does your current provider offer? Do you have an alternative? If these alternatives are only moderately viable, you will assign it a three or four. What other wants/needs do you have? What are the wants/needs and alternatives of your current provider? Make your best guess.

Leverage

Costs of Not Reaching an Agreement

Party	Strength of Want/Need — Wants/Needs	(1–7 scale, where 7 = strongest)	Viability of Alternative — Alternatives	(1–7 scale, where 7 = most viable)
You				
Your Current Provider				

Who do you think has greater leverage at this point?

___

Now, take another look at Table 7-1, back in Chapter 7. What are the techniques that you feel will be most useful in helping you increase your leverage?

Most Useful Techniques to Increase Your Leverage

___
___

Which techniques will be most useful in helping you decrease the other party's leverage?

Most Useful Techniques to Decrease the Other Party's Leverage

___
___

Reality Test

Okay, it's time to contact a long-distance telephone service provider. It can be your current provider or another provider. And you can contact a single provider or more than one company. Your objective is to get the best deal that you can from each provider. When you are done, write down the terms of their offer below.

Provider	Terms of Offer
1.	
2.	
3.	

Did you receive a better offer than your current long-distance plan? What inducements or sweeteners did they offer? More often than not, a better deal is possible.

Now let's look at how leverage changed during the negotiation. Who did you think had more leverage when the negotiation began? At the end? Which techniques did you employ (or try to employ) during the negotiation? Which were most successful?

Techniques I Employed	Degree of Success (1–7 scale, where 7 = very successful)
_____	_____
_____	_____
_____	_____
_____	_____

Why do you think that your most successful technique worked in this negotiation? Why do you think your least successful technique did not work so well?

Which techniques did the other party employ to change leverage? Which were most successful?

Techniques Employed by Other Party	Degree of Success (1–7 scale, where 7 = very successful)
_____	_____
_____	_____
_____	_____
_____	_____

Why do you think the provider's most successful technique worked so well? Why do you think his or her least successful technique did not work well?

If you did not contact more than one provider, you may have found it difficult to increase your leverage by focusing on alternatives because you did not have enough information about available alternatives to speak credibly. Remember, information is one of the central elements in negotiation. You can acquire information through secondary sources (for example, an organization's customers, competitors, or suppliers, as well as newspapers, magazines, and the Internet) or through primary sources (that is, directly from the other party). The more information you have in a negotiation, the better your chances of managing leverage and achieving success.

Finally, let's go back and examine the results of the "Negotiation

Reality Test

Techniques Questionnaire" presented earlier. Do you see any correspondence between the techniques that you employed in this reality challenge, or techniques that you applied most successfully, and the results of that questionnaire? Are there one or two techniques that you don't use as frequently or as effectively as you would like? If so, think about practicing the technique(s) in your everyday negotiations. It is through such conscientious practice that you will begin to acquire confidence and new skills.

13

> Diplomacy is the art of saying "nice doggie" until you can find a rock.
>
> —**Will Rogers**

Playing Defense

Thus far, we have been talking about ways in which you might increase your leverage or decrease the other party's leverage. As suggested by the long-distance telephone service provider negotiation just completed, there may be situations where you would prefer simply to neutralize or thwart the other party's attempts to gain advantage. You can, of course, follow the adage that the best defense is a good offense and go on the attack. Or, you can just play defense. How can this be done? Let's look at each of the eleven techniques, and how you might respond to the other party's use of each technique.

Matching His Products or Services to Your Wants and Needs

If the other party's technique is to match his products or services to your wants and needs, there are several options or countermeasures you can employ. One option is to be vague at the outset about what your wants and needs are. The other party will undoubtedly ask you some questions to learn more about your desires (for example, "How can I help you?" or "What are you looking for today?"). You might simply say that you are not sure or that you are just browsing. Alternatively, you can turn the question around (for example, "What's good today?" or "What's on sale?" or "What do you recommend?").

A good salesperson, however, will pay attention to your nonverbal cues, trying to gain a richer insight into your true desires. He or she may show you samples or suggest options as a way of learning more about the strength of your desires. You need to be careful about the signals you are sending.

The logic behind a salesperson asking questions—particularly open-ended questions—and keying on your nonverbal cues is to identify the product or service that most closely matches your criteria. The next step is to convince you that this is a perfect match. To counter this, you need to be prepared to point out where the imperfections are.

Altering Your Perceived Wants and Needs

On a recent trip to a jeweler to buy his wife a gift, a friend of mine was asked what he was interested in seeing. He said that he wanted to buy his wife some earrings for $100 to $200. The clerk said she had something special, and took him to a showcase to see some very attractive earrings. He said that he did, indeed, like them. She showed him to a seat and brought the earrings over. Then he saw the price: $700. He said his price range was $100 to $200. She put the earrings back in the showcase, went into the back room, and brought out a tray with several earrings on it. He saw a set that he liked, but when he asked the price he discovered the set was $450. He again reminded her of his price range. She brought out a second tray, where the price of most earrings was about $300.

If you have ever been to a jewelry store, you may not be surprised by this story. You enter the store with a set of criteria for a purchase, in this case three criteria: earrings, that satisfy your taste, for $100 to $200. The saleswoman tries not just to satisfy but to embellish your taste, albeit at the highest price she thinks you will accept. She is trying to alter your third criterion, and perhaps your second and first as well. By starting high, she may be able to convince you that $300 or $450 is a lot less than $700.

Salespeople are very adept at selling you something other than what you originally wanted or needed. A good car salesperson, for example, can get you to forget about the size or model or cost of the car that brought you to the showroom, and get you focused instead on the safety-lock features of a particular car. How do you counter this?

While there may, in fact, be an additional criterion for you to con-

Playing Defense

sider (so you want to be open to your unexpressed needs), more often than not you need to be true to your real wants and needs. You do this by giving some forethought to your criteria and prioritizing them. When confronted with a new criterion, you need to be firm in expressing what brought you to this store or person, and what will cause you to complete the negotiation. You can do this by telling the other party what you want, in so many words, or through nonverbal cues (looking away, frowning, moving to another item). If the behavior persists and you have other options, you may want to consider leaving the store altogether.

Tapping Your Affiliation Needs

Humans are social animals. The desire to be recognized, appreciated, and accepted is strong in most all of us. Consequently, that first question people ask themselves in any negotiation—"What do I want?"—often contains a relational component: I want you to like me.

Good negotiators will tap this affiliation need in a variety of ways. They will call you by your name (sometimes your first name, to indicate familiarity). They will compliment you on your clothes, smile, friendliness, wit, good taste. They will offer you coffee, ask you questions, listen to your stories, find things that the two of you have in common (sports, neighborhoods, travels, hobbies, and so on).

Because building a sense of relationship, if not a genuine friendship, is generally a good thing for negotiators, this initiative on the part of the other negotiator is not to be discouraged. However, the relationship building should be balanced or lean in your direction. So reciprocating with questions of interest, calling the other party by his or her first name, etc., is a good "countermeasure."

Sometimes the party who initiates these relationship-building behaviors can gain a perceived advantage by controlling the subsequent direction and flow or rhythm of the negotiation. For example, a buyer seeks to create familiarity, you reciprocate, and then she asks for something beyond your expectations (for example, a quantity discount). To counter this sequence, you may want to take control of the conversation and be the first to take action to build trust and friendship.

Individuals from Western countries sometimes find this to be the case in doing business in other regions of the world, where relational development is more extensive. The chief negotiator for an international hotel chain once advised against spending too much time developing friendships in international negotiations, as he saw this as a precursor to the other party asking for a favor.

Discredit Your Alternatives

The other party may try to discredit any alternatives you have to negotiating an agreement with him. He might do this as a preemptive measure, such as by pointing out the superiority of his product over a specific competitor's product. Or, the other party might wait until you mention an alternative and then seek to discredit it. The latter approach is more reactive than proactive, probably creating a negative halo for the other party.

In either case, you need to pay attention to the basis for discrediting an alternative. Someone trying to sell you encyclopedias may point out, for example, that their collection also comes with a subscription to a national magazine of your choice, which a competing encyclopedia does not. But if a national magazine was not something you originally wanted or needed, then it is not really a valid argument.

Whether or not the argument is true also is important. If the claim is false (for example, that no other encyclopedia offers a complementary national magazine), you may or may not want to challenge the assertion. Doing so risks turning the negotiation into a game of one-upsmanship, potentially embarrassing one or both parties. A more subtle response, sending a nonverbal signal that suggests you are uninterested, unconvinced, or see through the tactic, may be more appropriate (for example, changing the subject).

Eliminate Your Alternatives

In very competitive industries, where there are a small number of competitors and finite resources, one or more of the players may seek to reduce or eliminate your alternatives through mergers, acquisitions, and so on. On a national level, many governments seek to protect public welfare through laws restricting monopolies. To this end, they will not allow one company to control all or a major share of the airline traffic to a particular region, all of the radio or television broadcast stations in the country, or all of the pharmaceuticals market. Monopoly was the issue some years ago in the famous Microsoft antitrust case, where Microsoft was under investigation for its efforts to restrict if not eliminate competition in the computer software industry.

Companies will occasionally try to accomplish the same outcome through collusion and price fixing. By meeting privately with their competitors to fix the price of certain products, these companies in effect eliminate any competition that might be available to customers (that is, they decrease customer leverage) by forcing a single, inflated price on the market. As previously noted, almost everything you can imagine has been the focus of a price-fixing scheme over the years, including music CDs, semiconductors, airline prices, vitamins, computer games, and genetically modified seeds.

Essentially, there are two points at which the technique of eliminating your alternatives can be countered: prior to a merger, alliance, or collusion occurring, and after the fact. To address this technique at the first point requires that you be well aware of the players, their familiarity with one another, and their proclivity (for example, reputation, ethics, pressures) for taking actions to reduce your alternatives. Clearly, the more players there are, the more difficult it is for them to work in concert to eliminate your alternatives. For example, in the auto repair business, there are often many different companies, a good number of which are independently owned. There may not be a professional association through which they might meet. Consequently, it might be difficult to get all these businesses together to agree to set fees or prices. Also, determine if there is a regulatory agency that oversees this industry, which might make companies more fearful of pursuing illegal monopolies.

If there are a small number of players, then conditions may be better suited for mergers or alliances. One countermeasure is to take preemptive action, forming your own alliance with one of the players. If, for example, a company needs to ally with two other companies in order to control the market, you form an alliance with one of the remaining two in order to prevent the elimination of alternatives.

These same guidelines apply in auctions. There is always a chance that the potential buyers in an auction will conspire to hold the price of an item down. The more players there are at an auction and the less organized they are, the more difficult it is for them to collude. In addition, there are a number of bidding methods that can reduce the probability of collusion, including the first-price, sealed-bid auction (in which bids are submitted in sealed envelopes and the item is sold to the highest bidder), the Dutch auction (which starts with a volume of items at a high price and lowers the price incrementally at predetermined time intervals, at each point offering to sell any or all of what remains to those offering to pay that price), and the reserve auction (where the seller has a reservation price that is kept secret, and no sale will take place unless a bid is made that exceeds the reservation price).[1]

Alternatively, you can choose to act after the fact (that is, after some form of monopoly or collusion has transpired). This may involve a more prolonged (and expensive) undertaking, seeking redress through court action. Such was the case for Netscape in its lawsuit against Microsoft, claiming that the latter had sought to extend its Windows monopoly to the Internet browser market in an attempt to lock out Netscape. The courts, in effect, ruled that Microsoft was in violation of antitrust laws when it did not allow Netscape the same access to Windows that was available to Microsoft's Explorer.

Sometimes you are forced to act after the fact as the result of poor negotiating on your part or underhanded tactics by the other party. For example, some contractors will ask for payment up front, or a portion of the payment with the remainder paid when the work is half completed. Then, the contractor will disappear, attending to other jobs. With all the money in pocket, the contractor has little incentive to give you immediate attention. If this is all the money you had budgeted for this job, the contractor has in a sense eliminated your alternatives. You are left with assertive options, such as urging or threatening the contractor, contacting a licensing organization or better business bureau, or starting a legal proceeding (for example, small claims court).

Feign Disinterest in Your Product or Service

As already noted, one tactic that a party might employ to decrease another party's leverage is to pretend not to be interested in the latter's product or service. What do you do to counter another party pretending to be disinterested in the car you are trying to sell, property you want to lease, or the date you want with him?

The more you know about the other party's style (for example, tendency to feign disinterest or bluff), the better position you are in to call his bluff with a bluff of your own. As a salesperson, this may involve politely asking if you can help and, when told by the party in so many words "no," you can simply say you are available if she has questions and go about other business. Attending to other individuals (in effect, feigning disinterest in this individual) also works, particularly if there are a number of other individuals available.

If you don't have information in advance about the other party, you may be able to discern a particular interest based on the amount of time she spends focusing on a certain item. Likewise, if the individual says that she is not interested but returns at a later time, this is a clear signal of interest.

Sometimes salespeople will try to create interest where it is suspect, or get the party to express his or her hidden interest. They might casually mention, for example, in moving away from the customer that this item is the last remaining of its type, or that the item of presumed interest is on sale for today only. Alternatively, a salesperson might bring other customers over to the item of interest as a way of creating some competition for the item. This happens during dating as well. Often a woman, for example, is viewed as more attractive or desirable by a man when he sees her with another man.

Identify Deficiencies in Your Product or Service

There are going to be occasions where the product or service that you have to offer does not meet all the specifications demanded by the other party. How you respond to the other party will depend in part on his motivations, and there are several types possible.

One type is someone who is trying to get you to offer concessions by pointing out deficiencies in your product or service. People who are in the business of selling a particular product are generally well equipped to respond to such an individual because they have encountered these issues from other customers and learned what to say in response. Their response could be that all products lack the deficient feature, or that there is some compensating feature that makes this product valuable. If you haven't had this kind of experience, you either need to get it (for example, by having a friend play the devil's advocate and tell you all that is potentially wrong with your product or service) or you need to run through in your mind the sorts of shortcomings that others might find in your product or service. Then, you need to think of what your response will be. This forethought is necessary for most of us because we are not fast enough on our feet to come up with a good response at a moment's notice. If, however, you are caught by surprise, you can ask the other party an open-ended question (for example, "Hmm, tell me more. Why is that an issue for you?") in order to buy time to think of a response.

A second type of person that falls into this category is someone who genuinely knows what she wants and needs, and believes that what you are offering does not meet those needs. Some of the same techniques will work with this individual: pointing out that other products have the same shortcoming, or that there are other redeeming features of your product that more than make up for the deficiency. In addition, asking some type of open-ended ("Why?") question might give you insight into the reasons behind her belief. From this inquiry, you may discover another way of satisfying this party's underlying need or interest. Sometimes a salesperson will have something he can throw in as a sweetener or bonus that will help the individual get over this deficiency (for example, a product guarantee, an extended service contract, free delivery).

A third type is the party who always wants more and is never satisfied. It is almost like a game: For every explanation that you offer, there is another problem or deficiency pointed out. They don't seem interested in working together toward a common goal.[2] One way to deal with such an individual is to respond to all the deficiencies and, at some point, confront the person politely regarding his intentions. You would do this by changing the tone of your voice, pointing out that the product or service is a good value, and then being silent to allow the other party to respond. In doing so, call the person by his first name. If he is just testing you or trying to demonstrate his skills in product evaluation but down deep is really interested in buying your product, this person will change his approach. If he had no intention of completing an agreement, he will probably end the negotiation. If the latter happens, you have lost little or nothing because there was probably never any chance of an agreement. But remember, you want to break the cycle in such a way that you leave the door open to the other party to respond . . . and to do business with you in the future.

When the Other Party Expands the Purpose of Their Pursuit

A fairly sophisticated technique in negotiating is to reformulate one's situation by moving from a specific position to a recognition of underlying interests or needs (which open up additional options). How do you counter someone expanding the purpose of her pursuit?

Imagine, for example, that you are a professional house painter. A couple negotiating to hire you to paint their house suddenly realizes that it is not simply an issue of how much it will cost or what type of job you will do, but there are other factors such as the mess this job creates around the building and the paint fumes. This realization causes them to broaden the scope of their problem, from how do they get you (the painter) to give them a fair deal on this task to what are the other ways of protecting their house while minimizing inconvenience and cost over time. Your potential employers may begin to consider another set of potential solutions, including the idea of having aluminum siding installed. Aluminum siding only has to be installed once, there are no paint fumes, there is no maintenance involved, and the cost over time is lower than the cost incurred of repainting every three to five years.

Most of us are not very adept at this type of cognitive reformulation. We get locked into a product or idea, and it becomes an all-or-nothing proposition. The natural emotion associated with negotiating contributes to our inability to expand the purpose of our pursuit. Nonetheless, there are occasions where the other party will do so. Because this is likely to occur in a moment of inspiration, you may not see it coming. And unless the individual verbalizes this revelation, you may not be aware of the reasons behind his change in behavior.

Fortunately, in most cases the individual will make this realization known to you. The way to handle this technique is similar to the previously mentioned technique involving deficiencies in your product or service. First, you are wise to have given this some forethought, anticipating not only what deficiencies your product has, but what other products, including products that solve a broader set of concerns, are available and their strengths and weaknesses. Second, you might consider asking an open-ended question about the new solution (aluminum siding) as a way of getting at some of those other concerns that lie beneath the surface of our consciousness (messy yard, paint fumes). This may allow you to mold your product or service to the person's wants or needs.

Identify Your Competitors

Identifying your competitors is a simple and subtle way for an individual to attempt to decrease your leverage. As previously noted, this technique can be brought about by mentioning the name of the competitor, demonstrating that one has the names of competitors through newspaper ads, or asking you about your competitors.

There are two types of people you will encounter who use this technique. One type is the person who is just beginning their search for a particular product or service. You are the first qualified person they have approached, and they may hope that their search ends with you as they are not motivated for an extended search. The more information of this type you can glean from her either verbally or through reading body posture, vocal tones, and so on, the easier it will be for you to respond. If the individual is just beginning her search and does not necessarily want an extended search because the item of interest is a small-ticket item, you might take them on a vicarious search . . . a search that leads them back to you. For example, suppose you work in a paint store and someone comes in looking to buy a specific color of paint to touch up wood trim in her house. Your store is particularly busy at the moment, and when this individual finally gets to the front of the line, you inform her that the paint is not a standard color and will have to be mixed. To keep her from running off to another store, you might point out that very few if any stores will carry that original color. In addition, if she had some paint left over from when the trim was originally applied, it probably would not match because the painted trim has darkened with age. So, wherever she goes it will require mixing and matching. However, it should only take about ten minutes.

There is another way that negotiators will respond to this technique, particularly if more is at stake. This is not a tactic that I advocate, but I present it here in case you have it used against you. Suppose, for example, that Sara wants to buy a new car. She goes to a dealership, the first in a series she plans to visit, and the salesman shows her a car that she likes. She tells him that she likes the car, but that she would like to visit some other dealerships before deciding. He tells her that, if she comes back, she should be sure to see him personally, because he thinks he can get her the car for under $30,000. After visiting a host of other dealerships, Sara finally realizes that no one can sell her this car for under $30,000, so she goes back to the original salesman. He greets her warmly, Sara says that she is interested in the car, and he goes into a back room to get the final approval from his boss. But the boss won't allow him to sell the car for under $30,000, offering a handful of excuses. Tired from a day full of shopping, Sara may just decide to buy this car anyway. She has just been lowballed.

Lowballing is a tactic whereby someone offers a product or service at a price well below market. The individual never intends to close the deal for that price, but knows that no one else can match it so the other party will probably come back at some point to do business. Again, it is not a tactic that I advocate, but you should be aware of it.[3]

The second type of person who uses the identify-your-competitor technique is trying to get you to budge on something (for example, price). This is a tactic. By showing you that they are aware that you have competitors, they are hoping to nudge you into making a concession. And generally speaking, it is a bluff. If, for example, they have already been to some of your competitors (and this is a good thing for you to try to learn) and they are still talking with you, then there must be something about what you are offering that appeals to them. It may be the style of merchandise you have, your reputation for quality and dependability, or your convenient location. But there is something appealing about doing business with you. Otherwise, this person would be going somewhere else.

Generally, this individual is looking for one final assurance before he will complete the deal. It could be that he wants an assurance that you are confident in the superiority of your product or service. It could be that he wants someone to remind him of the feature your product has that other products do not have. So, you have to know what makes your product or service special, differentiating it from what your competitors carry, and reaffirm that feature. That is, in an objective, matter-of-fact voice, you might note that your competitor carries some fine products, but their models do not have heated seats or side-panel airbags.

Create Viable Alternatives

An ingenious negotiating counterpart may seek not only to signal that there are potential alternatives available to her, but to bring them to life as well. Generally, this type of creative energy is not wasted on small pursuits. That is, someone who is unhappy with the price of lemonade being sold during Fourth of July holiday parades is unlikely to decide to go into the lemonade business herself. It is simply not worth the effort. However, if the situation is one where a lot is at stake (for example, the financial viability of someone's company) or is prolonged or recurrent, the probability increases for an industrious and creative individual to create viable alternatives. How do you defend against such an action?

First and foremost, recognize the pressures that the other negotiator is facing. Be aware of whether or not the conditions are sufficient to move this person to create viable alternatives. To what extent have your prices become prohibitive? How long has this been going on, and how long is it likely to continue (in the mind of the other party)? What are the costs and benefits for the other party in seeking to create a viable alternative?

Companies that see their supplier's leverage increasing to the point where they feel at risk will sometimes buy the supply company or create their own such operation. This is what is known as vertical integration. A distributor of electrical energy decides to buy one of the hydroelectric plants that provide it with the energy that it distributes, thus eliminating the leverage of other hydroelectric companies.

Second, to what extent does a viable alternative readily exist? If you are aware of an alternative, the other party is likely to be aware or soon to be aware as well. Has the other party hinted at other options? Is he just beginning to shop for an item, or is the search well under way?

Perhaps the best way to deal with the other party creating viable alternatives is preventive action. Recognize the conditions that might lead the other party to take such dramatic actions. From time to time, offer them a break on price or offer to throw in a bonus or sweetener. They will most likely look forward to this occasional benefit, and be less likely to turn their attention to creating alternatives. As the saying goes, an ounce of prevention is worth a pound of cure. In this case, once the other party has begun to invest in creating a viable alternative, it will take a lot more to dissuade him from continuing with that pursuit than it took to begin the action originally.

Feign Other Options

There may be circumstances in which the other party pretends to have other options that do not actually exist. If you believe his or her options are real, then you may be inclined to make a concession.

This sort of bluff requires several elements to be successful. First, there is the believability of the option or alternative. The more you know about your product, service, or business, including your competitors and their products, the easier it will be for you to know whether or not the purported alternative is viable. Knowing that your counterpart's supposed alternative is not viable, it is probably advisable to simply communicate your knowledge indirectly rather than to challenge the other party directly on her veracity. For example, you might say "Mm-hmm, you could do that," showing that you know the option is not real or practical. It allows the other party to save face, which is important if you want to complete the current transaction or a future negotiation with her.

Whether or not the fictitious option is known to you, the other party must still be able to convince you through her acting that the option is real. Detecting a bluff based on nonverbal cues and select statements is no easy task, even for the most skilled individual. However, if you know the person who you suspect is bluffing, you may be able to recognize significant differences in her behavior. The person's behavior is different from past encounters, perhaps in part because she realizes how difficult if not futile it will be to try to deceive you and the implications of it.

You may recall an episode of "Seinfeld" in which a mutual friend of George and Jerry named Gary (played by Jon Lovitz) had been faking an illness. Gary reveals this to George, who has to promise not to tell Jerry. Because George and Jerry have been close friends for many years, Jerry can tell immediately that George knows something, although neither was able to discern this secret from Gary's behavior. Jerry says "You look like something's on your mind," which George denies stiffly. "So, that's your poker face," Jerry counters. George claims it is his regular face, but Jerry firmly contends that it isn't: "I've seen your regular face. That is not it." Jerry continues his assault, trying to ascertain how big the secret is, by asking George if he has (in poker parlance) a pair of bullets (two aces), two of a kind, three of a kind, a flush, and finally a full house. With each stronger poker hand, Jerry's voice gets more shrill and George gets more nervous. Finally, George caves and reveals the secret.

If you do not have a history with the person who you suspect might be bluffing, then you must use other means. Needless to say, it is much more difficult to accurately detect a lie or deceit under such circumstances. Research on lying and deception suggests that, in general, such individuals tend to speak more slowly, include more pauses in their speech, and stutter more. They may speak in a voice that is slightly higher pitched. Their impressions often appear to be rigid, planned, and rehearsed, resulting in less body movement, which was the case for George. Their statements are often negative, indirect, and lacking in description of personal experiences. They may include fewer details in their statements (to reduce the chance of contradicting themselves), and they are more likely to describe events in a chronological order. By asking questions, you may increase the likelihood of one or more of these indicators being revealed. But keep in mind that these are general guidelines, and not every individual will conform to these patterns.[4]

Finally, you can always call the other party's bluff with your own bluff. You can pretend that you have other customers or other business to which you must attend, you can pretend that there are others interested in the same product or service, you can pretend that you are indifferent to the transaction altogether. For example, if you are selling your boat, you might say that you are not sure if you really want to sell it. You might keep it, or give it to your daughter. As with the other party, the closer your statement is to reality and the better you are at bluffing, the more convincing your countermeasure will be.

Notes

1. For more on auctions, see the following Web site: http://pages.stern.nyu.edu/~akambil/teaching/cases/auction/flowerscase.pdf

2. This type of person reminds me of the type of individual captured in the Brazilian expression *amiga da onça* (friend of the jaguar). Someone asks you what you would do if you were out walking and you saw a jaguar. Your response is that you would head in the other direction. What if the jaguar followed you?, the person then asks. You say you would start running. What if the jaguar started running? You respond that you would climb a tree. What if the jaguar started to climb the tree? Hey, you respond, whose friend are you anyway, mine or the jaguar's? *Amiga da onça* means a false friend. And someone who keeps finding deficiencies in your product or service seems like an *amiga da onça*.

3. This tactic is similar to an advertisement in which a very low price is prominently displayed to grab your attention. Upon closer in-

spection, however, you see that the price has restrictions or the price is five times that amount (for example, 5 × $19.95).

4. For a good review of lying and deceit, and how to detect dishonest behavior, see A. Vrij, *Detecting Lies and Deceit: The Psychology of Lying and the Implications for Professional Practice* (New York: John Wiley & Sons, 2000).

14

> The test of a man or woman's breeding is how they behave in a quarrel.
>
> —GEORGE BERNARD SHAW

THE CLIMATE OF NEGOTIATION

As a number of examples have suggested, leverage can be gained by giving the impression that you can help the other party in some way, or that the other party can be hurt by not dealing with you. There are, in fact, four ways this can occur (Figure 14-1). These four ways create different climates or moods in a negotiation.

One form this can take is the introduction or offering of something

Figure 14-1. Forms of leverage and their consequences.

	Introduction	Removal
Pleasant Item or Event	Positive Reinforcement	Omission
Unpleasant Item or Event	Punishment	Negative Reinforcement

pleasant or desirable to the other party, whether this be a job, an item for purchase, or friendship. This is called positive reinforcement, since it presumably increases the likelihood of a desired behavior on the part of the other party. In addition, this form of leverage generally leaves the other party with a good feeling about you.

A number of the techniques of leverage discussed earlier take this form. For example, the techniques for increasing your leverage by focusing on your counterpart's wants or needs fall into this category. Certainly this is the case for tapping affiliation needs, since you are building a sense of relationship and creating rapport by calling someone by their name, asking about their family, friends, or hobbies, sharing common experiences, etc. It is also true for matching your products or services to your counterpart's wants and needs as well as for altering your counterpart's perceived wants and needs. Both techniques involve helping to satisfy the other party's desire or need, and often require a line of inquiry (open-ended questions) to determine what that need is.

Removing something that is negative (costly, undesirable, unpleasant) is called negative reinforcement. Do not be fooled by the term, as negative reinforcement is not punishment. Anything that is a reinforcer in behavioral terms increases the likelihood of a behavior being repeated. Positive reinforcement accomplishes this by introducing something desirable, such as by offering to throw in a video if you buy an exercise machine today; negative reinforcement accomplishes this by removing something undesirable.

To illustrate, imagine that your neighbor has sometimes seemed annoyed by the loud music you play on your stereo. By offering to turn the volume down, you remove something unpleasant. Similarly, if you have ever shoveled snow from your neighbor's sidewalk, worked the holidays for a coworker, or overridden a late fee for a customer who was delinquent with an account, you have been exercising negative reinforcement.

This is a subtle form of leverage because your service or favor may cease if the other party does not behave in a way that is acceptable to you. If, for example, you need a ride to the airport, your coworker may recognize that you may not work holidays for him in the future if he does not agree to take you. Thus, it is the potential loss of negative reinforcement (your willingness to free him from weekend work) that gives you leverage.

As with positive reinforcement, the techniques for increasing your leverage by focusing on your counterpart's wants or needs apply to negative reinforcement. By recognizing that your neighbor has a cold that prohibits her from shoveling snow, or that she simply hates cold weather and snow shoveling, you put yourself in a position to remove the burden of an undesirable task. You may even be able to talk your neighbor into this. For example, you point out what a cold day it is, a great day to stay inside and watch television, and then you offer to shovel her sidewalk, or you offer to cover for a coworker scheduled to work that weekend. In doing something that she finds unpleasant, you create, in her, good feelings toward you, just as with positive reinforcement.

Punishment, on the other hand, involves introducing something that is undesirable or negative. In this case, the term is used very broadly to include the threat of such actions as well. When you threaten to quit if your salary is not increased, when you suggest that you might buy from a competitor, and when you say that you don't like an artist's work, you are exercising a form of punishment.

There are a number of techniques that might be categorized as punishment. All of the techniques that relate to decreasing a counterpart's leverage by focusing on your alternatives involve a type of threat or punishment, although some more so than others. Creating viable alternatives certainly represents a form of punishment, and so does feigning other options or identifying a counterpart's competitors. The latter represents an implied threat. Similarly, feigning disinterest in a counterpart's product or service and identifying product or service deficiencies, which are techniques for decreasing a counterpart's leverage by focusing on your wants or needs, also represent forms of punishment.

Sometimes there seems to be a fine line between negative reinforcement and punishment. For example, J. Edgar Hoover was appointed the head of the Federal Bureau of Investigation (FBI) in 1924 and remained in that position until his death in 1972 at the age of seventy-seven. Franklin Roosevelt supported legislation to give the FBI and Hoover authority to use wiretaps to investigate domestic fascist and Nazi groups, and in the process Hoover was able to amass private information on all types of individuals. In time, this included information on President John Kennedy's liaisons. Hoover told Kennedy straight to his face that one woman was making an unusual number of telephone calls to the president's secretary, but that the affair the two were having was safe with Hoover. Obviously this information could be used against Kennedy at any time (punishment), but appeared to be framed almost as negative reinforcement.[1]

Omission is the final form of leverage. Omission involves removing something that is pleasant or desirable, or at least the threat of doing so. Examples include a company deciding to eliminate "casual Fridays," an airline eliminating its frequent flyer program, or a friend who stops calling you. Omission is similar to punishment in that it generally creates bad feelings.

Although techniques for increasing your leverage often involve positive or negative reinforcement, techniques that focus on your counterpart's alternatives can result in omission. Specifically, eliminating your counterpart's alternatives through mergers or alliances removes feasible alternatives. While this may have desirable consequences for you (for example, by expanding your market share), it limits price competition and potentially the choices available for customers. It also can affect employees and their unions, such as when two companies merge and some positions are cut.

One of the consequences of creating negative feelings through punishment or omission is that the other party may choose to end the negotiation and the relationship, or to reciprocate. Since one of the four characteristics of leverage is that it is relationship-based, ending the relationship effectively eliminates any possibility for leverage.

Reciprocal behavior is another possible outcome of creating negative feelings through punishment. This was illustrated in the dialogue involving an appliance store salesman and a customer presented earlier. Take another look at the dialogue, focusing on the mood of the negotiation.

SALESMAN: *Can I help you, sir?*

CUSTOMER (without giving eye contact): *No, that's okay. I'm just looking.* [Feigning disinterest]

SALESMAN: *Excuse me, please.* (walks off in the direction of another customer) [Creating viable alternatives]

CUSTOMER (after some time browsing, finally makes his way to the area of the washing machines, where the salesman also happens to be): *Hmm.*

SALESMAN: *Are you interested in washing machines?*

CUSTOMER: *Oh, I'm not sure. This machine does not have a time-delay feature, allowing you to program the start and stop times.* [Feigning disinterest, Identifying product deficiencies]

SALESMAN: *No, this model does not.*

CUSTOMER: *Carson Appliances carries Kenmore, which has that feature.* [Feigning other options]

SALESMAN: *Excuse me, please.* (leaving to attend to another customer) [Creating viable alternatives or Feigning other options]

All of the techniques used in this exchange represent a form of punishment, which can produce negative feelings. This may represent a low-key example of reciprocation, but it illustrates the point: Little or no movement toward resolution or agreement seems apparent, and neither party appears to be positively inclined toward the other.

Over the years, negotiation, conflict, and reciprocity have been studied rather extensively. The results suggest that negotiators are generally quick to offer tit-for-tat. That is, negotiators will reciprocate their counterparts' cooperative (win-win) behavior by disclosing information about their preferences and priorities, as well as reciprocate their counterpart's competitive (win-lose) behavior by withholding information or introducing misleading information. Negotiators also will match communication patterns (for example, multi-issue offers, threats, concessions), procedural statements (expectations for how the negotiation will be conducted), and statements or acts of emotion (positive or negative).

All of this makes choosing the appropriate form of leverage and specific techniques critical to managing the tone of a negotiation and the direction it will take. How can one exercise leverage while at the same time not be negatively affected by its application? And what factors determine which approach to take?

Note

1. When Lyndon Johnson became president, Hoover was about to reach the mandatory civil service retirement age. However, Johnson had the retirement age waived for Hoover, an indicator of both their friendship and Hoover's leverage.

15

> He makes people pleased with him by making them first pleased with themselves.
> —Lord Chesterfield

Selecting an Approach

There are several factors that determine the type of situations a negotiator can face and the approach or techniques that are best employed. These factors include:

1. One's relationship with the other party (short term or long term)
2. The importance of the negotiation (low, moderate, or high)
3. Whether or not one is able to anticipate the situation (Figure 15-1)

Challenging a parking fee, for example, is an unanticipated and relatively unimportant negotiation with someone with whom you are not likely to have a long-term relationship. A business merger, on the other hand, is both an important and anticipated negotiation with a long-term business partner. Thus, developing and maintaining a good relationship is essential.

Different types of situations are likely to call for different approaches to managing leverage. If you think about leverage in the mechanical sense, these different approaches represent levers available to you in any negotiation. Given this choice of levers, it is natural to wonder which approach makes the most sense. Are you better off looking for ways to increase your leverage, trying to decrease the other party's leverage, or both? And what lever would you use if you were interested

Figure 15-1. Types of negotiating situations.

	Short-Term Relationship		Medium to Long-Term Relationship	
	Low to Moderate Importance	High Importance	Low to Moderate Importance	High Importance
Anticipated	Hotel Check-Out Time Overdue Library Book Discount on Purchase	Home Purchase Business Acquisition Car Sale	Neighbor's Dog in Your Yard Son/Daughter Won't Eat Vegetables Employee Consistently Late to Work	New Job Salary/ Benefits Business Merger Conceiving Another Child
Unanticipated	Unappetizing Dinner Purchase Incorrect Change Parking Fee	Missed Flight Auto Accident Personal Theft IRS Audit	Dining Invitation Late Payment (e.g., rent) Offer to Carpol (co-worker)	Marriage Proposal Unexpected Pregnancy Poor Performance Evaluation

in increasing your own leverage? Would you focus on your counterpart's wants and needs, focus on his alternatives, or both? And if you chose to decrease the other party's leverage, would you be better advised to reduce your desire for his goods or services, increase your alternatives, or both?

Generally speaking, negotiators are more likely to pursue a single approach at any one time than multiple approaches simultaneously. This has been illustrated by several of the examples already presented—an advertising agency seeking to show a prospective client that it has the creativity to launch the client's product (increasing demand), a security firm reducing a potential client's alternatives with information about a competitor's impending bankruptcy (decreasing alternatives), and the public utility executive decreasing the leverage of a railroad company by physically linking up to a competing railroad's tracks (creating an alternative).

This is not to say that a negotiator cannot use multiple approaches, especially at different stages in the negotiation. The advertising agency, for example, might first try to increase the potential client's demand for its services, and later in the negotiation seek to marginalize a potential competitor. This combination approach was employed by London and Paris, the odds-on favorites in the competition to host the 2012 Summer Olympic Games. As the competition for hosting the games was coming to a close, the British team criticized a stadium in Paris, calling

Selecting an Approach

it unsuitable for the Olympics. French President Jacques Chirac, in turn, commented on the poor quality of English food and the trustworthiness of people who have such lousy cooking. Nevertheless, negotiators often exhibit preferences over time and across situations that represent a primary strategy or style for managing leverage. Which style or approach is the most common among negotiators and, more importantly, which is the most effective?

Any time you attempt to change the perceived advantage in a negotiation you run the risk of upsetting one or more of the parties. With some individuals this may not matter: The negotiation represents a one-time business proposition and you do not expect to see this individual again. However, in most cases you are negotiating with someone with whom you will have future dealings—a husband, wife, son, daughter, parent, in-law, neighbor, boss, colleague, customer, supplier, etc. What approach should you use with such a person?

There has been a limited amount of research in this area, but the anecdotal and empirical evidence points to using techniques for increasing your own leverage if you are interested in building or maintaining the relationship. Increasing your leverage, either by increasing the other party's demand for what you have or by decreasing the alternatives available to the other party, will generally increase the total dependency and cohesion in the relationship, while decreasing the other party's leverage will typically decrease dependency and cohesion. Thus, the importance of building or maintaining a relationship with the other party is key to determining which approach to use.

An individual seeking to buy a new computer directly from the manufacturer might feel comfortable trying to decrease the manufacturing representative's leverage by identifying product deficiencies or by feigning other options, approaches that decrease cohesion. The buyer is not likely to meet or even have contact with the representative again, so there is no relationship to create or maintain. On the other hand, someone interviewing for a job might not want to use these approaches, as he or she creates a negative mood and decreases the cohesiveness of the relationship. The former approach—identifying product or service deficiencies—suggests that the organization has deficiencies that make it a less-than-ideal workplace, while the latter approach—feigning other options—does likewise (as well as potentially creating distrust). Therefore, if building or maintaining a relationship with the other party is important, then seeking to increase your leverage, such as by focusing on satisfying your counterpart's wants or needs, is often preferred over seeking to decrease your counterpart's leverage.

It should not be surprising that techniques that involve increasing one's leverage by focusing on your counterpart's wants or needs are among the most common. Most of our social encounters, in our personal and professional lives, are with individuals with whom we have long-term relationships. Therefore, we most often seek to increase our leverage in this way in order to preserve or maintain these relationships. The techniques for doing so fall into the category of positive reinforcement, while many of the techniques for decreasing the other party's leverage correspond to punishment.

Of the two ways to increase your leverage (that is, either increasing the other party's demand for your goods or services or decreasing the other party's alternatives), increasing the demand for your goods or services is more common. Increasing demand is perhaps the most efficient technique to enact (certainly more efficient than creating new alternatives or eliminating a counterpart's alternatives through a merger or acquisition) while engendering the least negative feelings (certainly less than discrediting the other party's alternatives). Simply by asking "How may I help you?" you demonstrate concern or interest. To minimize the negative feelings often associated with focusing on a counterpart's alternatives, a negotiator either has to be very skilled in the social arts of discrediting alternatives and feigning disinterest in a product, or has to employ a third party (for example, a lawyer) who can absorb the negative feelings potentially associated with these techniques. In the case of the 2012 Olympic bid, both London and Paris undoubtedly lost some international respect for their attempts to discredit the other city as a viable alternative.

Increasing demand for goods or services by matching your products or services to your counterpart's wants and needs, altering his or her wants and needs, or tapping affiliation needs requires its own set of skills. These include quickly building rapport where no prior relationship exists, having knowledge of your counterpart's likely interests (for example, based on customer groups to which he or she belongs), asking open-ended questions to elicit additional information, and being able to read nonverbal cues throughout the encounter. These are all skills that any highly effective salesperson has mastered.

What are your skills and preferences? Go back to the questionnaire

Selecting an Approach

you filled out in Chapter 7, and the scoring table for that questionnaire. Which of the two primary approaches to altering leverage had the higher point total—increasing your leverage or decreasing the other party's leverage? Which focus within that approach is your preference—focusing on wants or needs or focusing on alternatives? Which technique(s) received the most points? Least points?

Table 15-1 displays the scores of a sample of 254 individuals, 58.3 percent males, and ranging in age from 17 to 80 (mean age = 37.7). As can be seen from this data, decreasing a counterpart's leverage (82.3) was marginally preferred over increasing your leverage (80.0). The most popular focus was increasing your leverage by focusing on a counterpart's wants or needs, and the most popular technique was matching your products or services to a counterpart's wants or needs, followed closely by expanding the purpose of your pursuit. The least popular was feigning disinterest in a counterpart's product or service. How do your scores compare with these?

When the data were broken down by age and gender, younger respondents were found to be statistically more likely than older respondents to increase their leverage by focusing on a counterpart's alternatives (more specifically, discrediting other alternatives), and to decrease their counterpart's leverage by identifying his or her competitors. In terms of gender, males were more likely than females to employ techniques for increasing their own leverage. Specifically, males indicated they were more likely to focus on a counterpart's alternatives, and more likely to try to discredit or eliminate a counterpart's alternatives.

It is important to understand your own tendencies, as well as those of others (which can be countered using some of the techniques described in Chapter 13). As with all tactics and behaviors, having some flexibility in your choice of approaches and techniques is invaluable. Equally important is how you apply a technique.

Table 15-1. Typical use of techniques for altering leverage.

Interest	Focus	Techniques	Technique (21)	Focus (63)	Interest (126)
Increasing Your Leverage	Counterpart's Wants/Needs	Match your products/services to counterpart's wants/needs.	16.9		
		Alter counterpart's perceived wants/needs.	13.2		
		Tap affiliation needs	14.9	44.9	
	Counterpart's Alternatives	Discredit other alternatives.	11.2		
		Eliminate counterpart's alternatives (e.g., through merger or alliance).	11.3		
		Combination of these two techniques.	12.5	35.1	80.0
Decreasing Counterpart's Leverage	Your Wants/Needs	Feign disinterest in counterpart's product/service.	10.4		
		Identify product/service deficiencies.	13.6		
		Expand purpose of your pursuit.	16.1	40.2	
	Your Alternatives	Identify counterpart's competitors.	14.3		
		Create viable alternatives.	14.2		
		Feign other options.	13.2	41.9	82.3

Sample consists of 254 respondents, 58.3% males, with a mean age of 37.7 years (range: 17 to 80).

16

Give me a lever long enough and a fulcrum on which to place it, and I shall move the world.

—Archimedes

The Art of Communication

A successful negotiation has been described as one in which you get everything you want, and the other party feels good enough about the exchange that he or she would choose to negotiate with you in the future. Perhaps it should go without saying that if you take advantage of the other party, and this individual becomes aware of this abuse, the individual is at the very least not likely to want to negotiate with you again. And if you reveal questionable or unethical tactics early in the negotiation, you also may not get what you want; your negotiating counterpart will likely become resentful, suspicious, and stubborn about allowing you any headway in accomplishing your goals.

Leverage and Distance

There is something to be said, therefore, for maintaining some distance from one's efforts to gain or exercise advantage. This, in fact, was suggested in the second chapter of the book, during the discussion of the meaning of leverage. Recall from that chapter the following definition for leverage: The distance of the direction of a force from the axis or lever is sometimes called the leverage of the force.

Distance has its advantages. There are mechanical reasons for adding distance, as the claim by Archimedes suggests, but there are also social or behavioral advantages when it comes to negotiating. Imagine, for example, the situation where one of the individuals in the real estate company that you founded has not been meeting sales targets for residential properties. This has been going on for some time, despite the fact that other salespeople are performing well. You could confront this individual yourself, but there may be some resentment, even if it is done privately. Alternatively, you could ask the individual who manages the residential sales staff to do an analysis of sales performance for each salesperson. This comparative analysis creates an awareness of substandard performance through numbers rather than words. And the pressure that comes to bear on this individual now includes peers rather than just the manager or you.

This is not so dissimilar from what political figures do from time to time. When an event creates political fallout, top politicians will look for cover. They will find a fall guy and distance themselves from both the event and this individual. Or, they will find someone else to do the dirty work. This is largely the responsibility of the press secretary for the president of the United States, but it may also fall to an aide or undersecretary.

At the 2004 Republican National Convention, the Republicans didn't choose George W. Bush, the presidential candidate, or Dick Cheney, his vice president (who had been coming under fire for hard-line decisions), to lead the attack on the Democrats. Rather, they chose Zell Miller, a Democratic senator from Georgia, to play the pit bull and attack the character of Democratic candidate John Kerry. This brilliant political move got the message out, and kept the beneficiaries of the message clean. How could Democrats or the electorate blame Republicans, since it was a fellow Democrat who led the attack? Thus, by choosing to have someone else apply the leverage, you are less likely to "get your hands dirty" (as Archimedes might if he was too close to the earth when he attempted to move it).

Or to put it another way, if it is obvious to the party who is being leveraged that the force is coming from you (for example, because you are telling them directly and explicitly what will be lost if there is no agreement), then the costs to this party have changed. True, it is quite clear to the other party from your statement what they will lose if no agreement is reached. But now there is ego involved as well, because of the direct and explicit way you presented your case. Thus, there are transaction costs. It costs the other party something in self-respect or pride if he accedes.

Colin Montgomery, an exceptional European golfer who has not always enjoyed the same success on the U.S. professional golf circuit, has come to be the target of some fans. Although every professional golfer experiences the occasional camera click or verbal jab at an inopportune time, Montgomery has taken obvious offense to these intrusions. His responses, both verbal and nonverbal, have only served to encourage unsportsmanlike behavior from one or more fans. Alternatively, other golfers have chosen to ignore these comments, or to employ their caddies or event officials to act on their behalf. By instructing their caddies or officials to take action, these golfers maintain some distance from the act itself.

There are several ways to distance yourself from the person with whom you are trying to gain leverage. Four of them are described below.

1. *Authority Limits.* With this tactic, you claim that you need to check with another individual (your boss, partner, etc.) before you can close the deal. Frequently, this person wants an additional concession or two. You may or may not have actually checked with this person (in fact, in some cases the person does not even exist), but by ascribing any additional demands to him or her, you create distance between yourself and the demand.

2. *Good Guy–Bad Guy (or Good Cop–Bad Cop).* Similar to authority limits, this tactic involves a two-person team, where one person plays the good guy and the other person plays the bad guy. In a buyer-seller negotiation, for example, the bad guy pretends not to like anything about a particular product. The good guy pretends to ally with the seller, needing just a concession or two to convince the bad guy to go along. In essence, the bad guy is the authority limit.

3. *Engage Another Individual to Act on Your Behalf.* In applying leverage, this individual effectively becomes the messenger. And as we all know, it is the messenger who takes the blame. Through a third party or "agent," the flow of communication also works to your advantage. Your agent is likely to reveal little information regarding your wants and needs, while the other party is more likely to react with emotion and provide valuable information.

As an exercise, try negotiating on behalf of someone else. That is, ask a friend if there is a negotiation, though not necessarily a critical negotiation, which you can conduct for him or her. It might involve returning an overdue video, buying a small appliance, or making a hotel reservation. How does it feel to play this role? How might you have behaved differently if you had been negotiating for yourself?

4. *Communication Medium.* When we think of negotiation, we often imagine face-to-face communication, but there are a number of other media that can be employed, including videoconferencing, telephone conversations, voice mail, text messaging, e-mail, and letters to create distance. These media vary in terms of their inherent level of information richness (Figure 16-1).

Face-to-face communication is generally considered the richest medium of communication. It allows for both verbal and nonverbal information to be shared, the latter containing far more information about intentions. Face-to-face communication also allows the other party to ask for clarifications and feedback, which improves the richness of the information. Videoconferencing has many of the same features as face-to-face communication, although some aspects of nonverbal communication may not be available due to the resolution or limited scope of the camera. Electronic mail, which has become a central medium for

Figure 16-1. Communication media and information richness.

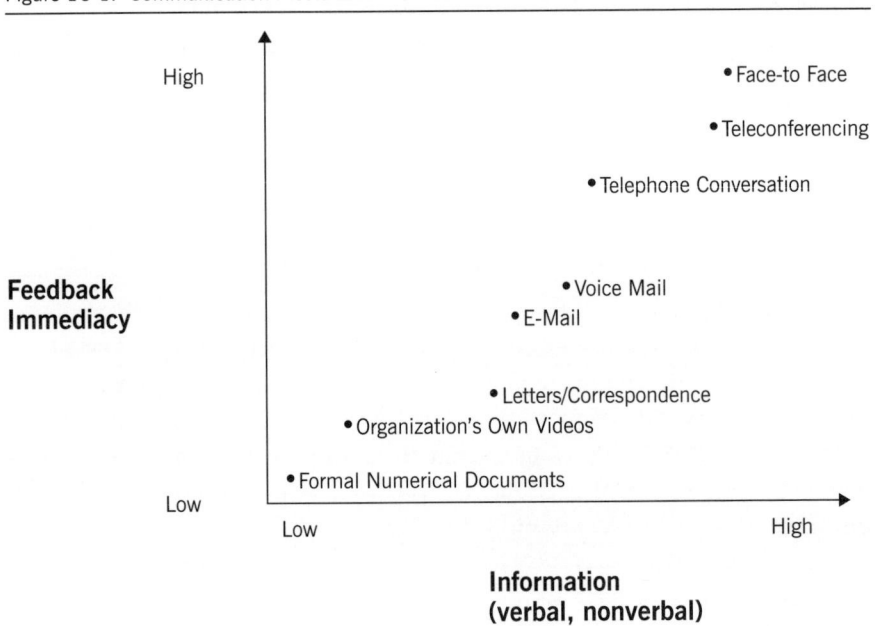

Feedback Immediacy (vertical axis: Low to High)

Information (verbal, nonverbal) (horizontal axis: Low to High)

- Face-to Face (High feedback, High information)
- Teleconferencing
- Telephone Conversation
- Voice Mail
- E-Mail
- Letters/Correspondence
- Organization's Own Videos
- Formal Numerical Documents

both personal and professional communication, has moderate information richness. (Perhaps the modest information richness of e-mail messages is one reason why teenagers these days seem to prefer that medium for chats over face-to-face meetings or even telephone calls. Much of the self-consciousness of that age group is masked by the medium.) A single document or letter is generally low in information richness.

Imagine a situation in which you are not a very confident negotiator. You are negotiating a deal that is very important to you, and you believe that the other party represents your only true available option. If you fear that your lack of confidence or inexperience as a negotiator is likely to lead to the other party learning that you have few if any alternatives, you may not want to employ a medium that is very rich. To attempt to negotiate face-to-face, for example, may result in the other party learning the perceived importance of the deal for you and your lack of options. Leaving a voice message may be preferred. Making a call and leaving a message, or sending an e-mail message, also suggests that you are possibly too busy to make a personal appearance. This communicates leverage as well.

Levels of Interaction

Should you choose to employ face-to-face communication to exercise leverage, there are different ways in which you can engage the other party, some more direct than others. These levels of face-to-face interaction, shown in Table 16-1, also have implications for managing leverage, whether enacted by you directly or by another party on your behalf.

Level One: Explicit. The most direct form of interaction, Explicit Interaction involves open verbal communication about an issue in question. In the situation described at the beginning of the chapter, where you are the founder of a real estate firm, you might go directly to the underperforming salesperson and say: "You have not made any sales in the past two months. If your performance does not improve, we will have to replace you."

Level Two: Verbal Tacit. Verbal Tacit involves communication that is superficially about something else, but really intends to express something about the matter in question. For the situation above, you

Table 16-1. Four levels of interaction.

		Examples	
Level	*Description*	*Identifying Counterpart's Competitors (house purchase)*	*Identifying Product Deficiency (mattress purchase)*
Explicit	Open Verbal Communication About the Matter in Question	"Sorry, but I have to leave. I have another house to visit."	"This mattress is not very firm."
Verbal Tacit	Talk that is Superficially About Something Else, But Really Intended to Express Something About the Matter in Question	"There are a lot of houses for sale in this neighborhood."	"How many coils do mattresses generally have?"
Behavioral Tacit	Behaving in a Way Intended to Implicitly Convey One's Feelings	Checking out newspaper's real estate section, with circled ads.	Pushing down on mattress to demonstrate lack of firmness.
Implicit	Individual Unconscious of How His/Her Words or Actions Are Meant to Influence the Other Party	Looking at house across the street with "For Sale" sign.	Not being able to easily get off (out) of soft mattress.

Based on: V. Daniel's "Communication, Incentive, Structural Variables in Interpersonal Exchange and Negotiation."

might say to the underperforming salesperson: "A number of our competitors are laying off staff because of declining revenues." In all likelihood, the salesperson will deduce from your message that declining revenues lead to layoffs and the parties contributing least to the company's revenues are most likely to be laid off.

Level Three: Behavioral Tacit. With this approach, an individual behaves in a way that implicitly conveys one's feelings, but does not necessarily express those feelings in words. For example, as founder of the real estate firm you might post sales figures for each salesperson in the conference room. By showing each person's contributions and the total shortfall for the company, you send a message that things must change, and if revenues don't, salespeople will.

Level Four: Implicit. This approach involves an individual being unconscious of how his or her actions might influence the other party. For example, in meeting with the underperforming salesperson, you sit behind your desk rather than around the coffee table with this individual. You may not even realize that you are doing this, but because of your frustration with this individual you distance yourself from him.

Recall earlier that we indicated one technique for decreasing your counterpart's leverage was by identifying his competitors. As a prospective homebuyer, this can be done in an Explicit way by saying something like the following: "Sorry, but I have to leave. I have another house to visit." Or, you can employ a less explicit approach, such as by saying "There are a lot of houses for sale in this neighborhood" (Verbal Tacit) or by checking out the newspaper's real estate section (Behavioral Tacit).

Self-Test

Let's see if you've got it. Imagine the following: You hold the rights to a patent that is potentially being violated by all of the major auto manufacturers. While patent infringement is always subject to legal interpretation, your lawyer thinks that you have a good case. You have been meeting with one of the auto companies in an attempt to form an alliance. You would like to bundle your patent with two of their patents to strengthen your case. They will provide the financial backing to pursue lawsuits against the other auto manufacturers, and in return become co-owners of the patent.

After three months of meetings, the agreement has appeared ready to be consummated several times only to lose momentum over a legal technicality, scheduling problem, or a change in personnel. Most of the meetings have involved your lawyer, and she has occasionally acted alone on your behalf. You are now thinking of pursuing other options if the agreement cannot be signed very soon. Using each form of interaction described above, how might you communicate your intentions of pursuing other options (manufacturers) in a meeting with the auto company executives? What would you say or do, using each form of interaction?

Explicit:

Verbal Tacit:

Behavioral Tacit:

Implicit:

The Art of Communication

Which would you feel most comfortable employing? Least comfortable? Which do you think would be most effective? How would you use your lawyer in closing the deal?

There are, of course, many ways of enacting each of these four forms of interaction. For example, you might tell the auto executives directly that you are going to pursue an agreement with another manufacturer (Explicit), casually mention that you met one of the executives from a competing company last week, and he said to say hello (Verbal Tacit), open your card folder, which reveals business cards from other auto companies (Behavioral Tacit), or, when the auto executives hesitate to finalize the agreement, you quickly pack up your things (rather than your customary probing for the reasons behind their reluctance), thank them for their time, and leave (Implicit).

In general, the Explicit form of interaction is likely to create the least distance between you and the message. In other words, it is a short lever that could produce some negative feelings toward you, depending on how it is delivered. For example, if you tell the auto executives directly that you are going to pursue an agreement with another manufacturer, they may view your statement as a challenge or ultimatum. The other forms of interaction are more indirect and subtle, allowing the other party to act on their own accord rather than because you forced the issue.

Think about how you send your face-to-face messages, and which media you prefer to use in your negotiations. As always, having flexibility as a negotiator is important. If you feel there is one or more of the forms that you need to add to your repertoire, you may need to practice them one at a time in your everyday negotiations. The following challenge will help you get started.

17

> Experience is what you get when you didn't get what you wanted.
>
> —**Italian Proverb**

Another Reality Challenge

Let's try applying some of these concepts to a real situation, one that most of us have found ourselves in at one time or another. Only this time, we are going to create the situation in order to practice these communication concepts. The situation involves returning an item to a retail store.

Most stores have policies regarding whether or not they will accept returns. Some stores will not accept items under any circumstances; purchases are final. Other stores will accept a return, but only up to a certain period of time following purchase (for example, thirty days). Still other stores will accept return items, but will only give store credit, not cash. Some will charge you a restocking fee. Finally, most stores require you to have a receipt as proof of purchase. No receipt, no returns.

Identify a recent purchase that you would like to return, an item that can be found in other stores. If you do not have a recent purchase that you would like to return, you can purchase an item for the purposes of this exercise, saving the receipt. For simplicity sake, you may want to select an item from a supermarket, such as a box of kitchen trash bags, aluminum foil, or dishwashing detergent (preferably something nonperishable, unless you want a real challenge). It should be a national brand rather than a store brand. Your challenge is to return this item to a different store than the one from where you bought it, *without the receipt*.

Before you begin this challenge, let's do an analysis similar to the one we did earlier in the book to assess who has leverage (that is, the costs of not reaching an agreement for each party).

Costs of Not Reaching an Agreement

Party	Strength of Want or Need (1–7 scale, where 7 = strongest) Wants/Needs	Viability of Alternative (1–7 scale, where 7 = most viable) Alternatives
You		
The Retail Store		

Your answers to these questions may depend on a number of factors. For example, how long have you been going to this particular retail store, how well do they know you, and what would be the cost to them of losing you as a customer (lost business, friendship)? Another factor concerns the financial condition of the store, which might be a function of how long it has been open, its location, its competition, and economic conditions generally. If the store is doing well, increasingly popular with little competition, and in fact quite busy much of the time, the customer service representative may perceive that he or she has alternatives to satisfying a single patron's concerns, particularly if it involves bending the rules. If the store is near one or more other stores, which are equally or even more attractive places to shop, you have alternatives.

Related to the issue of the general financial condition of the store

Another Reality Challenge

is the size of the retail store. Some stores are part of a larger chain, and therefore can afford to accommodate customers in this way. There are supermarket chains, for example, that sell organic products at higher prices and create an appealing environment by offering samples of fruits, breads, cheeses, and prepared foods. They bend over backwards to provide a variety of customer service amenities, which they build into their price structure. An independent store may not have the volume or profit margin to be able to absorb a lot of returns.

This analysis may cause you to rethink to which store you want to return the purchased item. The goal of this exercise is not to find the easiest path to follow (that is, the store that has the most lenient policy regarding return of purchased items). The goal is to practice some new behaviors in a real, live setting.

Given this background and challenge, what are some ways that you can increase your leverage? That is, what are some ways that you can increase the costs to the other party of not having an agreement? One way might be to go to customer service with a cart full of items to purchase. In fact, you could have the clerk ring up all the items, and just before giving him your credit card, ask about returning the product purchased elsewhere. This technique falls into the category of matching your products or services to your counterpart's wants and needs—he wants you to purchase all those items, he does not want to have to restock them (some of which may be perishable items), and he does not want to have to void this sale (which may require a supervisor's key). Keep in mind, however, that you run a risk in doing this, as the customer service representative may wonder if you simply pulled an item off the shelf and are attempting to get money for it. In addition, some stores have a separate counter for returns.

While the items are being rung up, you could also strike up a conversation with the customer sales representative about how you always end up buying so much more than intended when you shop at this store. This also falls into the category of matching your products or services to your counterpart's wants and needs. By striking up a conversation with the customer service representative, calling her by her first name, you tap into affiliation needs.

You can also think about ways to decrease the leverage of the other party, although this is already in your favor. In other words, think about how you can decrease your costs if an agreement is not possible. Because there are undoubtedly other stores where you can attempt to return the item, you have alternatives. And since you have the receipt to this item and can return it at any time to the store where you bought it, you have the ultimate alternative. Knowing this will make you more relaxed in your negotiation.

Okay, now let's focus on the four levels of interaction—Explicit, Verbal Tacit, Behavioral Tacit, and Implicit. Sometimes it is worth rehearsing, if only in your mind, how you might approach the other party in a negotiation. How might you engage the other party, using each level of interaction? What specifically might you say or do? Write your ideas below.

Explicit:

Verbal Tacit:

Behavioral Tacit:

Implicit:

The Explicit level of communication is perhaps the easiest to imagine. You can simply say "I would like to return this item." You can

Another Reality Challenge 135

communicate the same thing in a Verbal Tacit way by saying something like "I am always buying things I don't need, or that I already have" and presenting the item. Or, when you first go up to the customer service counter, you ask: "Is this where we return items?" It is a bit more difficult to imagine commencing the item return in a Behavioral Tacit or Implicit way, although these can be used later in the negotiation. You can put the item on the counter after all your purchases have been rung up, or simply put the item on the counter if you have no purchases. But it seems like you are going to have to say something.

There is a good possibility that the customer representative will ask for a receipt. What do you say or do then? At the Explicit level of communication, you might simply say "I do not have the receipt with me" (which is true). You could also, of course, say that you bought the item at another store. A Verbal Tacit response might be to say "This is one of my favorite stores. I shop here all the time. People are very friendly and helpful." A Behavioral Tacit approach might be to start looking through your purse or in your wallet or pockets.

Enough preparation. It's time to take the challenge. When you have tried one or two stores, let's meet back here for a debriefing.

Post-Negotiation Analysis

1. Were you able to return the item? _____

2. Which techniques for increasing your leverage did you employ? _____

3. Which techniques for decreasing the other party's leverage did you employ? _____

4. What techniques did the customer service representative employ? _____

5. Which of the levels of interaction did you employ, and how effective was each? _____

6. What forms of interaction did the other party employ, and how did you respond to each? _____

7. Do you think you were unethical in your approach to returning the item? _____

8. Overall, how would you rate your negotiation and your use of leverage specifically on a 7-point scale, where 1 = unsuccessful and 7 = successful? _____

If creating distance in applying leverage is important, you probably found that the Verbal Tacit and Behavioral Tacit approaches were most effective. They are less direct, less confrontational. Consequently, they are particularly useful in responding to another party's Explicit behavior, since they are less likely to create negative feelings and reciprocal behavior.

At the same time, distance in social leverage is more likely to lead to misunderstanding and, potentially, ineffectiveness. The other party may not make the connection between your looking down at your supermarket basket full of groceries and your intention not to purchase those items if the other item is not returnable. Behavioral Tacit and Implicit interactions are subtle.

Remember, the more you practice these techniques and levels of interaction, the more comfortable and effective you will become with each. In the days ahead, pay attention to those techniques you favor most in your negotiations, and those you favor least. Also pay attention to the techniques that others employ, and how you respond to each technique. If you can identify a technique that others are employing to which you do not have an effective response, you may want to identify an effective response from the chapter on "playing defense" and practice it a few times. All these techniques can be acquired through practice.

18

> The trouble is, if you don't risk anything, you risk even more.
>
> —Erica Jong

Leverage, Uncertainty, and Risk

In the movie *Kramer vs. Kramer*, Dustin Hoffman plays Ted Kramer, a young father whose divorcing wife wants custody of their son. Just prior to a hearing to determine who should have custody, Kramer loses his job in advertising. Desperate for a job immediately, he goes to an advertising firm during their Christmas party, urging them to view his work. When they say that they will get back to him in a few days, Kramer says no and begins to pack up his portfolio: "This is a one-day-only offer, gentlemen. You saw my book. You know I can handle the work. I am willing to take a salary cut. The only thing is, you're going to have to let me know today, not tomorrow, not next week, not at the end of the holidays. If you really want me, you make a decision RIGHT NOW."

Negotiation involves uncertainty and risk. Risk occurs when one acts on the probability that a certain event will occur in the future. For Hoffman's character, there was a very high probability that he would lose custody of his son if he did not have a job, a probability close to 100 percent. Uncertainty exists when the probabilities are not precisely known. It is unmeasurable risk. For example, Hoffman's character had no way of knowing how his very explicit demands would be received. As it turned out, he got the job.

Because most of life's decisions involve some degree of uncertainty or imperfect information without a guaranteed outcome, we all take risks. Generally speaking, our willingness to take a chance is deter-

– 137 –

mined by how we view a situation in terms of likely gains or losses (Table 18-1). People are more likely to take risk when there is a moderate- to high-probability of losses or when there is a low-probability for gains, and they are less likely to take risks for low-probability losses or for moderate- to high-probability gains.[1] This would explain the behavior of Hoffman's character: There was a high-probability that he would lose custody of his son if he did not get this job, while at the same time a low-probability of his being hired on the spot by this advertising firm (particularly in the middle of their holiday party). Consequently, he gave the advertising firm an immediate deadline. This was an extreme risk, since he was presumably down to his last option. And he revealed the magnitude of the risk by showing both disbelief and gratitude when they called him back into the office and announced that they would hire him.

The more information one acquires, the less uncertainty exists about the probable outcome of an approach or decision. This includes knowing another party's style and how they are likely to respond to your tactics, as well as knowing the cost to the other party of not having an agreement (wants/needs and alternatives). A risk-averse individual is likely to gather more information than a risk-taking individual.

Your preference for one or more of the eleven techniques or for one of the four forms of interaction may signal an orientation toward risk. To tell someone that you are going to pursue an agreement with his competitor (Explicit interaction), particularly when no such partnership is in the offing, requires more risk taking than asking questions to uncover the other party's real needs. It also requires more risk taking than thanking the individual for his or her time, packing your materials, and leaving. The latter represents Behavioral Tacit or Implicit interaction, which leaves much to the imagination of the other party

Table 18-1. Communication and control.

	Risk Averse	Risk Taker
Outcome:	Low-Probability Losses; Moderate-to-High-Probability Gains	Low-Probability Gains; Moderate-to-High-Probability Losses
Information:	Highly Valued and Sought	Not Highly Valued and Not Sought
Evaluation:	Absolute Terms	Relative Terms
Approach:	Decrease Other Party's Leverage	Increase Your Own Leverage

and which you can later deny. This is the nature of nonverbal behavior: It can be easily misinterpreted and its intent, therefore, denied.

Similarly, the "distance" you create between yourself and the party you are trying to influence also can reflect your risk-taking propensity. Someone who lacks self-confidence or who is concerned about public image may be less inclined to confront another party directly. Instead, he or she will work through other parties (for example, subordinates, agents).

Research on risk taking and negotiation suggests that individuals who have a high risk-taking propensity are likely to employ more aggressive tactics that are self-oriented, are likely to make fewer concessions, are likely to take chances regarding outcomes. In contrast, individuals with a low risk-taking propensity are more likely to cooperate with the other party.

While it is important to understand your own orientation toward risk, it is equally important to understand your counterpart's orientation. To the extent that risk is situation specific, you have some control over the other party's behavior. You can shape his or her view of a situation, which can influence your counterpart's willingness to make a decision in your favor or desire to withdraw to collect more information (and reduce his or her perceived risk).

If you want the other party to decide immediately and in your favor, you want him to perceive the situation as one involving moderate- to high-probability losses and low-probability gains. A real estate developer who talks with a carpeting company about growth in the condominium market and plans for other developments, while at the same time alluding to other carpeting companies with whom they have contacts or could contact, is increasing the perceived probability of a loss for the carpeting company if it does not offer a good price and prompt service. Under such circumstances, the carpeting company is more likely to be risk seeking and make a hasty decision, rather than delay and gather more information (for example, about the likelihood of future condo developments and the viability of the real estate firm doing business with other carpeting companies). At the same time, if the carpeting company thinks that they are the frontrunner and that the contract is quite lucrative, they might bid low for the job. That is, they would be risk averse regarding how much to ask for the job, because they are faced with high-probability gains.

Risk-taking orientation is likely revealed in another aspect of negotiations. In assessing the potential costs involved in any given situation, a negotiator can take one of two viewpoints. The negotiator can view these costs in absolute terms, or she can view them in relative terms. In viewing a negotiation in absolute terms, the negotiator merely looks at the costs that she is likely to incur if an agreement cannot be reached. Alternatively, the negotiator can view her costs relative to those costs likely to be incurred by the other party. Which party stands to lose more?

Consider again the scenario, described in Chapter 6, in which you had an automobile accident on your way to a meeting. In this scenario, you failed to stop in an assured clear distance. You can view your predicament—more points on your license, potential loss of license, higher insurance premiums—in absolute terms and offer to pay the other party substantially to keep the police from filing a report. Or, you could consider that the other party, likely driving under the influence of marijuana, has more to lose if the police are called. Thinking in relative terms, you would find ways to make the other party aware of his potential costs (jail time) and, ultimately, pay little or nothing for your failure to stop.

In general, an individual who consistently thinks in absolute terms, even when he or she has a large relative advantage in terms of potential costs, is risk averse. In contrast, someone who always sees things in relative terms is more likely to be a risk taker. It is possible for someone who thinks in relative terms to mistakenly see a favorable differential, even where one does not exist. This would lead to foolish risk taking. However, the individual who can assess a circumstance in absolute and relative terms will often be able to recognize a clear advantage in terms of costs, and be in a better position to exploit his or her advantage. This individual will seek to illuminate the other party's potential costs in a situation where the costs are comparable, causing the other party to accede.

The notion of relative costs applies in multiparty situations as well. Consider, for example, the situation where your boss is asking for someone to work the upcoming holiday weekend. There are five people in your department, and all five have received the e-mail message from the boss. If you choose not to volunteer, there are certain costs that you might incur (for example, your boss's disappointment and challenge to her power). However, you know the situation for several of the other members of the department, and two of your peers are very interested in receiving employee-of-the-month awards. You are not interested in such recognition. Therefore, the cost to them of not agreeing to volunteer for weekend duty is much greater than it is to you. In absolute terms, the costs to you remain the same. But in relative terms, your costs appear marginal.[2]

Because a risk-averse individual is likely to see things in absolute terms, focused on personal losses, he is more likely to look for ways to decrease those potential losses or costs. This means that a risk-averse individual is more likely to try to decrease the other party's leverage by feigning disinterest, identifying product deficiencies, identifying competitors of the other party, or feigning other options. A risk taker will try to increase his own leverage. Dustin Hoffman's character in the movie *Kramer vs. Kramer* was a risk taker who gathered almost no information about his potential employer, sought to match his skills to the prospective employer's needs, and effectively eliminated at least himself as an alternative if he was not immediately hired.

Of course, not everyone falls into these two categories—risk averse or risk taker. Many of us fall somewhere in between. In addition, our orientation toward taking or avoiding risk can change over time. The more one has to gamble, whether it be money or social capital, the more one often is willing to risk.

However, as suggested by Erica Jong's observation that opened the chapter, there is likely greater risk in not taking any risks at all. There is, indeed, some risk in seeking to fully live and enjoy life itself.

Notes

1. A. Tversky and D. Kahneman, "Advances in Prospect Theory: Cumulative Representation of Uncertainty," *Journal of Risk and Uncertainty*, 1992, 5, pp. 297–323.

2. This is reminiscent of the humorous story of the two guys who are out in the woods hiking. All of a sudden, a bear starts chasing them. They climb a tree, but the bear starts climbing up the tree after them. The first guy gets his sneakers out of his knapsack and starts putting them on. The second guy says, "What are you doing?" He says, "I figure when the bear gets too close, we'll have to jump down and make a run for it." The second guy says, "Are you crazy? You can't outrun a bear." The first guy responds, "I don't have to outrun the bear. I only have to outrun you."

19

I regard him as a salesman.

—JAMES BARKSDALE

LEVERAGE AND ETHICS

It should be obvious from many of the preceding examples that leverage is a powerful tool in negotiation. A natural question, therefore, is how much leverage should someone have before entering into a negotiation, and by what means? If you enter into a negotiation with leverage, when is it appropriate to increase your leverage? Are there times when you should decrease your leverage, or at least the perception? And are there certain techniques or tactics that would allow you to gain advantage in a negotiation that would be considered unethical (for example, the lowballing tactic)?

Recall the challenge you were given earlier, to return an item without a receipt to a store other than the one where you bought the item. This exercise causes some individuals consternation. Part of that uneasiness comes from being put in an unusual situation; it is not every day that you return something without a receipt, which feels to most individuals like asking for a favor. But another part of the discomfort comes from a sense that returning this item to a store other than the one where you bought it is unethical. When pushed to explain why it is unethical, several different reasons are offered: it is extra work for the cashier, the store has to restock the item, it creates inventory problems, or the item is "used." Of course, the issue of ethics might also depend on what you say during the negotiation. If you lie and say that you bought the item from the store when you did not, it can create some personal angst. If you say you lost or forgot the receipt, those are lies as well.

In fact, in a court of law such behavior could be considered fraudulent and subject to prosecution, although a minor act of this sort is not likely to be pursued. Fraud is a technical term that describes an event consisting of five elements. An act is considered fraudulent if it is:

- Intentional.
- A misstatement.
- Of a material fact.
- Relied upon by the other party.
- To the other party's detriment.

Let's assume that you did not make any misstatements of fact, including that you did not say that you would like to return the item since you were technically not returning it as you bought it elsewhere. Instead, you simply asked for credit for an item that the store carries. This is not fraudulent, but is this unethical? Certainly the store has a choice in the matter. There are reasons, good reasons in their mind, for taking the item back. For starters, they might capture you as a new customer.[1]

What if you do not make any false statements, but are nonetheless deceptive? For example, the clerk asks if you bought the item at this store, and you respond "Not this particular store," suggesting that you bought it at another store that is part of the supermarket's chain. Or you deflect the question with an oblique statement: "This is my favorite store." Is this unethical?

If you tell the store representative that the item was purchased elsewhere, a form of full disclosure, is the negotiation now unethical? What if you have a cart full of groceries? What if you did not intend to use the full cart as a technique to gain leverage? Is this unethical?

Ethics refers to the principles, norms, and standards of conduct governing an individual or group. It is derived from the Greek word "ethos," which means custom or tradition. Therefore, what is considered ethical is what is considered customary by a defined group of individuals. How one defines the reference group is one of the factors that makes ethics difficult. Depending on whether the reference group is one's friends, family, workplace, city, state, country, or region, a dif-

Leverage and Ethics

ferent set of customs or traditions might apply. And customs change over time, albeit slowly, even within the same group of people.

The quote at the beginning of this chapter comes from Netscape CEO James Barksdale. During the Microsoft antitrust case, he was asked whether he considered Netscape co-founder James Clark to be a truthful man. His response, "I regard him as a salesman," suggests a special set of ethics for this group of people (that is, for this profession).

Herein lies one of the challenges of negotiation. How does one proceed when dealing with an individual from a different group with a different set of customs? There are some scholars and policymakers who believe that we all belong to the same group, the human race. They would like to see a universal code of ethics that would apply in all business transactions. While there may indeed be a common code that can be established on certain issues, in reality we belong to many different groups that have overlapping but not identical customs. Further, when people are faced with negotiating challenges or obstacles, they will sometimes choose the reference group that allows them the greatest freedom of expression. So while a salesman may adopt one set of behaviors with his family, when selling his house he may choose to think in terms of what other members of his profession would or would not do.[2]

What if the other party has a different set of customs that include the use of tactics that your immediate reference group considers unethical? Certainly you have a right to defend yourself, no? How does one develop leverage in a situation where questionable or unethical tactics are being employed? Many times one party will take advantage of another party if they see the negotiation as one-time or episodic. But if you think of negotiation as being part of the fabric of life (personal and professional), linked or continuous rather than episodic, then you realize that a negotiation is never truly over until life itself is over. (Remember, leverage is relational.) You may encounter the person to whom you just sold your problematic car as your waiter in the restaurant where you are dining, on the softball team you are playing against, or at the private club you want to join. Suddenly, you are faced with an awkward encounter, an extension of what seemed like a one-time negotiation. We all belong to many groups, some of which we have yet to join.

Several of the techniques described earlier involve what many believe to be questionable or unethical behavior. This includes feigning disinterest in a counterpart's product or service when you are really interested, and feigning other options when you do not have any. How do you feel about these behaviors? Do you consider them appropriate? Have you ever employed either?

Most individuals in Western societies would consider these fairly commonplace and acceptable, particularly the former behavior. Feigning disinterest could be executed without risking a declaration or statement of fact (for example, through nonverbal behavior). The latter—feigning other options—might require a false statement, so this could be seen as less acceptable.

Some of the other techniques, however, might be considered equally inappropriate. Eliminating a counterpart's alternatives, for example, represents an act of assertiveness if not aggression. Even techniques such as discrediting the other party's alternatives or identifying product or service deficiencies would make it onto some individuals' lists of inappropriate behavior.

If your standards regarding what is appropriate behavior are higher than those of others, this will limit the techniques you will employ. It may not restrict your counterpart, however. He or she may use some of these techniques, or put you in a compromising position by asking you to do something illegal or unethical, such as paying a kickback in order to get a contract. How, then, can you negotiate effectively? You have several options.

Managing Ethics

Some people will change their standard in the face of a less-than-ethical negotiating counterpart, and feel quite justified in doing so. This might be viewed as an act of self-defense or tit-for-tat, acceptable in many cultures. There is, in fact, some research that suggests individuals will alter their ethics when they feel the other party is playing by a different set of rules, whether it be exaggerating opening offers or paying a bribe to gain an advantage. Individuals who do this may be enlarging or refocusing their social grouping to include individuals who will use such tactics. However, what if you want to be true to your values?

The second option is to not negotiate with this individual. Remember, leverage is a relational concept, so by severing the relationship you remove the other party's power. This was discussed in relation to a scenario presented in Chapter 10, as you may recall, the case of the printing company owner who reneged on an oral agreement and handshake.

A third option is to detect the techniques the other party is using. That is, you can try to detect the lying or deception of the other party, and with the information attempt to change the balance of power in the negotiation or withdraw because the other party cannot be trusted. There are several ways of detecting a lie or bluff. The easiest and surest way is to know from a reliable source that your counterpart is prone to exaggeration or misrepresentation. This information may not tell you that a specific statement is false, but it is an indicator of what can be expected generally. The more you know about the conditions under which he or she lies (for example, with new acquaintances, with friends, in social negotiations, in business negotiations, one-on-one, in important negotiations, when up against a deadline), the better off you will be.

Alternatively, you might acquire information that could be used to test the other party's veracity during an encounter. Imagine, for example, that you are thinking of buying a used car and the dealership agrees to let you take the car for a test drive, during which time you stop at your neighborhood repair shop and ask the mechanic to inspect the car. Learning from the mechanic's trained eye that the car had been in an accident is information you can use in determining the salesperson's honesty. Along with a number of other questions, you might ask the salesperson if the car had ever been in an accident. Similarly, you can gain information before buying a house about rezoning plans, noisy neighbors, property tax increases, and so on, which might be used in testing the other party's forthrightness.

You can also, of course, try to "read" the other party's posture and gestures in an attempt to detect lying. This is far easier said than done. As previously noted, research suggests that liars tend to speak more slowly, include more pauses in their speech, and stutter more. Their impression often appears more rigid, planned, and rehearsed, with less body movement. Truth tellers, especially if emotional, are inclined to tell their stories in an unstructured way, whereas liars describe events in a more chronological order. A liar's statements are often negative, indirect, short on details, and lacking descriptions of personal experiences. These are general guidelines for detecting dishonesty, however, that may not hold in your particular negotiation. The better you know the other party, the better you will be able to spot anomalies in speech patterns.[3]

Some negotiators will use alcohol as a means of testing the other party's likely veracity. If the other party refuses to imbibe, it is not only viewed as unsociable but also a potential signal that this party is withholding information or has illicit intentions. Because even modest alcohol consumption can cause some individuals to lose their inhibition and divulge critical information, drinking is common in many types of negotiations (particularly international negotiations). (This then raises the question, of course, as to whether or not pushing alcohol to gain an advantage in a negotiation is ethical.)

Finally, there are a couple of things one can do to neutralize the potential unethical behavior of another party. An individual is less likely to act unethically if he or she thinks that there may be future business opportunities or if information regarding his or her behavior might get back to colleagues or friends. Thus, talking about future business opportunities and identifying individuals that are associates of the other party will help to neutralize unethical behavior. These actions relate to the operational definition of leverage given earlier: The more it costs the other party not to have an agreement, the more leverage you have. So if we think of agreement as something that spans more than a single negotiation, then not having an agreement that focuses on the needs and interests of both parties is going to cost the party acting unethically.

Notes

1. There is an urban legend regarding Nordstrom's department store, which has one of the most liberal policies regarding return items. Some years ago a man brought two snow tires to a Nordstrom's store for a refund, even though Nordstrom's is an upscale clothing store that does not sell tires. The clerk accepted the tires and gave the man a refund.

2. As a further illustration of the relative nature of ethics, consider the disaster in New Orleans caused by hurricane Katrina. Many individuals, stranded and without food or water for days, looted stores for essential items. Was this considered ethical? Some people said it was not, but many others deemed it appropriate behavior under the cir-

cumstances (although they differentiated between taking food and taking televisions).

3. There is a fascinating game called "Mafia," which tests one's skills in detecting deceit. The game requires no special cards, board, or facility, and is great fun. For a detailed description of "Mafia," see Appendix A.

20

> It's my rule never to lose my temper till it would be detrimental to keep it.
>
> —SEAN O'CASEY

MANAGING EMOTIONS

A young man needed to replace the batteries in his electronic organizer. The characters displayed on the organizer screen were fading, so the batteries needed to be replaced quickly. Otherwise, the information stored in the organizer would likely be lost. Busy at work, he called a nearby store, which did not carry the special lithium batteries. He called a second store, Radio Shack, but the clerk asked for his phone number to call him back. An hour later, the clerk still had not called. So the man took a bus to the Radio Shack store, angry that he had not received a call. He approached the counter, and asked one of two clerks about the batteries. They were quickly located, very near the counter. He asked the other clerk, who was waiting on a customer, why he did not call him back. The young man was told that the store was busy. "Do you receive a commission on sales?" the young man asked the clerk. "Yes," he was told. "Then I want a discount on these batteries. I want your commission," he demanded. The two clerks said that they couldn't do that. "Then I want to see the manager," the young man countered. The manager was not in today, he was told, as one of the clerks began to ring up the item at the cash register. "Then give me the manager's name," he shot back. He was handed a business card with the manager's name on it, and he looked at the clerk who had not returned his phone call and wrote his name on the back of the card. "I am not buying those batteries," he said, turning quickly and exiting the store. Angry, he took the next bus back to work, where he got out the

– 151 –

phone book to find another store that might carry the batteries. In the yellow pages he saw a listing for Best Buy, a new store across the street from Radio Shack. He had forgotten all about that new store. He checked their Web site, and saw that they carried the lithium batteries. So he put his coat back on and went back outside to take the same bus back to the neighborhood where both stores were located. And he did, indeed, find and buy the batteries he needed at Best Buy.

Each and every one of us has been in situations like this, where we lost our composure. It might not have been lithium batteries at Radio Shack, but it was something similar—an item advertised on sale that was sold out, photos that were supposed to be developed in twenty-four hours that didn't come in, an automobile repair that didn't solve the problem, a sole-source supplier whose delivery was a week behind schedule. We get frustrated, upset, indignant, discouraged, or depressed, in part because we feel at a disadvantage. As a consequence, our emotions inhibit our ability to reason and we fail to take actions that will efficiently and effectively rectify the situation.

In an odd way, emotion is like water. Someone once said that the greatest source of headache for a homeowner is water. Water erodes foundations, weathers siding, backs up toilets, seeps through walls and roofs, leaks from pipes, freezes in pipes, and attracts termites. Yet it is essential to our existence. Our food depends on it. We wash our clothes and ourselves in it. Our septic systems require it. And it makes up the majority of the weight of a human body, 60 percent for the average adult.

What water is to homeowners, emotion is to negotiators. At some level, emotion is essential to all negotiations. Were it not for some level of emotion, we would not have any compunction to ask the restaurant hostess to validate our parking ticket, ask our friends to help us move, or ask a love interest for a date. Emotion is part of what motivates or drives us to get up in the morning and engage other human beings.

Yet emotion, like water, can also be the source of our problems. Too much emotion during a formal presentation can cause us to appear nervous and disorganized, forgetting important information. Too much emotion in a sporting event can cause an athlete to overpitch, overthrow, or overkick a ball. Too much emotion while driving on a busy highway can lead to dangerous behavior and accidents.

In negotiating, as in life, many different emotions are possible. In simple terms, the feelings associated with these emotions might fall

Managing Emotions

into one of the following categories: mad, sad, glad, or afraid. Each, in turn, has associated behaviors. When people are mad, they are inclined to shout, scream, use profanity, pound their fists, turn red, stop listening, lean forward, get closer, use threats, stop talking, or overwhelm another with words. The young man looking to replace the batteries in his electronic organizer exhibited some of these behaviors. When people are sad, they frequently stop listening, withdraw, stop talking, stop thinking, get sick, cry, drop eye contact, stop eating, or eat in excess. When people are glad, they very well might smile a lot, talk excessively, curtail thinking, grant favors, let issues slide, or buy you lunch. Fear causes people to stop listening, stop thinking, tremble, stutter, clam up, capitulate, avoid, or withdraw.

Can too much emotion be a bad thing in negotiation? Maybe. It depends on who has the emotion, under what circumstances, and what the emotion is. And it depends, of course, on the effects of the emotion. Being mad certainly did not work to the advantage of the young man looking for lithium batteries. It impaired his thinking to the point where he could not even recognize a viable alternative to getting the batteries at Radio Shack—simply walking across the street to Best Buy.

Because information is very important in negotiation, including and especially to the perception of advantage or leverage, by getting emotional you may lose control of some of your faculties (ability to observe, detect, reason). So might the other party, if he or she gets emotional. As a consequence, an essential technique like expanding the purpose of your pursuit (that is, moving from positions to interests or from wants to needs by asking "Why?") becomes almost impossible to employ.

Because of the effect of emotion on data gathering and thinking, individuals will sometimes try to raise the level of emotion to their advantage. If a party can't think of other questions or options, he or she might simply accept the offer on the table. Who is most likely to become emotional during negotiation and conflict, and who is most likely to be affected by it?

In recent years, there has been a surge in interest in what has come to be called emotional intelligence. Emotional intelligence is a form of social intelligence that involves the ability to identify, understand, and manage one's feelings and emotions, and those of others, to effectively handle potentially difficult situations. There have been a number of studies suggesting that higher emotional intelligence is associated with higher sales performance, better college grades, and professional success and prestige.[1]

While researchers and scholars are still learning about this form of intelligence, there has been an interest in determining whether females or males are more naturally gifted in this area. Early results suggest that overall men and women are equally intelligent emotionally, but in different ways. Women, in general, are more aware of their emotions, show more empathy, and are more adept interpersonally than are men. On the other hand, men, in general, are more self-confident, optimistic, adaptable, and they handle stress better than do women. One study, for example, found that when the level of anxiety was increased 25 percent for men and women negotiators, the likelihood of reaching an agreement dropped by 11 percent for women in the experiment but dropped by only 4 percent for men.

Cultural factors also can affect the expression of emotions during conflict and negotiation. In the United States, Canada, northwestern and central Europe, Australia, and New Zealand, for example, logical, rational argumentation is commonplace in negotiations. Consequently, individuals are likely to exhibit moderate emotion. In Mediterranean Europe and Latin America, the display of emotion is more central to argumentation and debate. Therefore, more emotion is apparent. In eastern Europe, the Middle East, and Africa, emotion also may be more apparent, although the argumentation will likely be more idealistic. In the Pacific Rim (excluding Australia and New Zealand), there may be little or no perceived emotion or argumentation. This is not to say that there is no emotion, only that it is not as readily apparent.

There are, of course, other factors in our genetic makeup and character, some based on life experiences, that determine how emotional we are likely to be, the types of emotion we are most likely to feel and express, and the circumstances under which these emotions will be most pronounced. Let's focus on the four emotions discussed previously—mad, sad, glad, and afraid. Are you the type who raises your voice, tries to overwhelm the other party with words, employs profanity? Do you stop talking, feel badly, start crying, and change your eating habits? Do you smile, get giddy, and become agreeable to everything? Or do you tremble, capitulate, and withdraw? Think about the sum

Managing Emotions

total of your negotiating experiences. Which of these three emotions are you most likely to feel? Which are you least likely to feel?

As the quotation at the beginning of this chapter suggests, perceived emotion is something that can be useful to you in a negotiation. If the other party is more likely to respond favorably to emotion, real or contrived, then you have a potential advantage. There are several possible reasons why the other party might respond to your advantage. One reason is because they are afraid of an affiliation loss. Another reason might be that they perceive you might be on the brink of pursuing other alternatives. If you had leverage at this time, this would cause them to fear that their wants or needs might not be realized.

We've all experienced emotion-based leverage. That is, we have all been in situations where the other party responded with sudden emotion or an exaggerated emotion that left us at a loss for words—a boss who pounded his fist on the desk, a customer who shouted, a friend who cursed like never before. It may have created such tension for us that we didn't know what to do or say.

As noted, one of the keys to effective negotiating, perhaps the most critical element, is information. If you know what the other party's wants and needs are and what alternatives are available to him, you have a tremendous advantage in a negotiation. If you know the basis for the other party's emotion, whether it is an important product delivery or a cultural characteristic, you have a better chance of maintaining your own emotional balance during negotiations with him.

Because face-to-face encounters spur emotion for most of us, which makes data gathering more challenging, it is probably to our advantage to learn as much in advance of the encounter as possible. The more we know, the better equipped we are to anticipate and interpret the other party's behavior. We are more likely to know, for example, if this individual will exhibit emotion, real or fabricated. We are more likely to know this party's true needs and available alternatives.

If the other party becomes unexpectedly emotional, however, you may be forced to adopt other measures. In such cases, acknowledging the emotion and then asking for clarification is often the best approach. Ultimately, your goal is to understand the needs that underlie the individual's emotions. If the emotions become overwhelming for both of you, asking for a break or recess to clear the air may be necessary.

Note

1. Although the study of emotional intelligence is relatively recent, there are already a number of questionnaires on the market claiming to measure emotional intelligence characteristics. At the time of this book's printing, www.queendom.com and www.testcafe.com/ei offer questionnaires on emotional intelligence. The questionnaires consist of fifty to seventy questions that will provide general information about your emotional intelligence, and more detailed information for a small fee.

> Information is pretty thin stuff unless mixed with experience.
>
> —Clarence Day

21

Negotiating in Cyberspace

To this point, the negotiation challenges you have been asked to take up have been either face-to-face (returning an item to a store without a receipt) or over the telephone (switching long-distance service providers). Despite the fact that electronic mail has only modest information richness, it has rapidly become one of the most popular forms of communication. Many negotiators will use it for at least some portion of their negotiations, particularly if the parties are separated by considerable geographic distance or one party is frequently traveling.

The following reality test is designed to provide additional experience using electronic mail as a medium. To get the full effect of this medium, it is recommended that you communicate asynchronously (exchanging e-mails over a period of days) rather than synchronously (communicating in real-time, such as in a chat room). In either case, you will want to use text only.

Although this may seem cumbersome, it actually has advantages for the young and inexperienced negotiator. The other party cannot see your youthful appearance and the nervous twitching you experience when backed into a corner. In addition, the asynchronous format slows down the negotiating process, allowing you time to reflect, check your notes, rework messages, and ask a friend for advice, among other things. It takes much of the emotion out of the negotiation.

To give you experience using electronic mail as a negotiating medium, a two-party negotiation simulation was created. This negotiation involves a bus company, Walloch Transportation, which recently expanded its route, and a fast-food restaurant, Brad's House of Burgers, with a restaurant along the new route. Because of the length of the new route, Walloch Transportation is looking to either build a bus stop or contract with a restaurant to use their facilities.

You will play the role of a representative from Walloch Transportation. You need to find a friend, colleague, or classmate who is willing to play the representative from Brad's House of Burgers. You might want to pick someone of the opposite sex to play the Brad's House representative. The roles for each representative can be found on my Web site: www.american.edu/academic.depts/ksb/management/volkema. At the site, you will see a list of contents at the top left, including a listing for Transportation Role Play. Click on this listing, which will take you to the links for the two roles. Please read only the background information for your role as the representative for Walloch Transportation. Ask the other party to go to the Web site and read only the role for the representative from Brad's House of Burgers. Each role has about one page of confidential information.

Be sure to save a copy of the transcript of your e-mail exchange. When you have completed the negotiation, return to this chapter to record the terms of your agreement and to process and debrief the experience.

Terms of the Agreement:

Debriefing

How did the negotiation go? Were you able to reach an agreement? How many e-mail exchanges did you have? Generally, this negotiation will take at least a half-dozen exchanges to reach an agreement.

How did it feel negotiating via e-mail? If you are like most people, you probably had mixed feelings. While you liked the luxury of being able to consult your notes, the pace of the negotiation may have frustrated you. In addition, while your own nonverbal cues were hidden by the medium, you were not able to read the face of the other party.

How would you characterize your emotions during this negotiation? Some negotiators get more anxious during an e-mail negotiation, particularly if the other party does not respond immediately or if the other party writes something upsetting. The lack of nonverbal cues and immediate feedback often raises questions about the other party's intentions. For this reason, it is generally advisable to meet face-to-face before turning to a medium with moderate information richness like electronic mail.

On the other hand, you may have taken comfort in knowing that the other party could not see your immediate reaction to an offer or demand. And you could "cool off" before responding to an upsetting message. Some people will, in fact, write a reply to a message and then set it aside for a day or so, rereading it to ensure that the tone works to their advantage before making modifications and sending it. Did you do this?

Who do you think had leverage at the beginning of the negotiation? Why do you think Walloch Transportation or Brad's House of Burgers had leverage? Did the leverage change during the course of the negotiation? Who had leverage at the end of the negotiation?

Go back to the transcript of your e-mail exchanges, perhaps even printing out a copy. See if you can identify the specific techniques for altering leverage that were used during the negotiation. Which of the eleven techniques did you use most frequently? Which techniques did the other party use? Generally speaking, did you try to increase your leverage in the negotiation or decrease the other party's leverage? Which approach did the representative from Brad's House of Burgers use more frequently?

There is some evidence that people will take more chances in terms of offering misleading information (such as exaggerating an offer or demand) or erroneous information (bluffs, lies, and so on) with a medium such as electronic mail. Do you think that you did so during this negotiation? What about the other party? As noted earlier, the lack of nonverbal cues makes it easier for a person to conceal his or her emotional state when acting unethically.

If you have not already done so, get together with the person that represented Brad's House of Burgers and share your perceptions about this negotiation. What do you think you did well in this negotiation? What do you think you should do differently next time? What did the other person do well? What should he or she do differently next time? Ask the other party to answer these questions as well, and then share your self-assessment of your performance before getting feedback from the other party.

Finally, how would you feel about doing business with this person in the future? Would he or she be willing to do business with you?

22

> A wise man knows everything; a shrewd one, everybody.
>
> —Anonymous

Multiparty Negotiations

To this point, most of the negotiations we have been talking about have been two-party negotiations. While two-party negotiations are not uncommon, particularly in personal negotiations, many professional negotiations involve additional individuals. In fact, sometimes negotiations that begin with just two individuals expand to include others. The auto salesman, for example, with whom you just reached an agreement, needs to check with his manager before the contract can be signed. Or the owner of a tool-and-die factory needs to consult with the head of the factory's union before selling the company to an interested buyer.

The participants in a multiparty negotiation always consist of the primary parties that "own" the problem or opportunity being negotiated (that is, the individuals who are directly affected by the agreement). These parties may represent themselves, or they may employ agents or other representatives. In addition, there can be colleagues or confederates of these parties who play a role in the negotiations. Most public policy issues attract a whole host of interest groups with a stake in the debate and its outcome. Consider, for example, the question of taxing purchases made over the Internet. There are numerous groups with a stake in this outcome, including Internet providers, Internet-based retailers, brick-and-mortar retailers, states with a sales tax, the federal government, and consumers.

Multiparty negotiations can involve as few as two sides, but often involve many more. Where there are just two sides involved, the negotiations are referred to as bilateral negotiations ("lateral" meaning side). Each side will generally have multiple parties. For example, most labor-management negotiations are bilateral, with management comprised of supervisors, managers, owners or shareholders, and the board of directors. When more than two sides are involved the negotiations are typically referred to as multilateral negotiations. For example, negotiations over a state's biennial budget would involve many sides with different needs and interests. Likewise, negotiations involving multiple countries seeking to form an economic union would be considered multilateral (for example, NAFTA, Mercosur, the European Union).

Sometimes it is not obvious how many sides are involved in a negotiation, or who all the stakeholders are. In the case of taxing Internet purchases, for example, shipping companies like Federal Express and UPS also have a stake in the outcome: Their businesses might be hurt if a sales tax results in fewer online purchases. Even in ostensibly simple negotiations, such as the purchase of a new automobile, there can be hidden parties. The buyer has a wife and teenage son who, while not present, have strong feelings about the type of car that is selected.

One of the biggest mistakes that inexperienced negotiators make in multiparty negotiations is to assume that there are fewer stakeholders than actually exist. This is a natural (and wishful) tendency because negotiations are perceived to be more manageable if there are fewer parties involved. It is often after a tentative agreement has been reached, however, that other stakeholders appear, reacting negatively to a process and outcome from which they were excluded. Having to reprise negotiations, given these new-found stakeholders, frustrates and angers those who were part of the initial process. Thus, one of the first rules in multiparty negotiations is to have all the people identified and represented who are necessary to reach a binding and lasting agreement.

The more people involved in a negotiation, the more issues likely to be in play. That is, when stakeholders are added to a negotiation, they will likely bring additional issues to be addressed and resolved. The owner of the tool-and-die factory may be primarily interested in negotiating the price of the company, the form and timing of payment (such as cash or stock), and his expected role in the organization over the next three years. The head of the union for the factory may be

Multiparty Negotiations

interested in whether or not the existing labor-management contract will be honored by the new owner, and ensuring that the workforce is not downsized. Community leaders want to be assured that the factory won't be closed or relocated. While you want all essential parties to be represented, you do not necessarily want all parties present. Imagine the chaos if every tool-and-die employee and community activist showed up for this negotiation.

Figure 22-1 illustrates four types of situations a negotiator can face, depending on whether there are a few issues to resolve or many issues to resolve. It also incorporates the effects of emotion in a negotiation when the issues are divisive. A simple negotiation, relatively speaking, involves only a few issues and the issues are not divisive. For example, you are planning to go to dinner with a friend or associate, and you need to negotiate the time and place you will meet. In a conflictive situation, there are only a few issues, but one or more of them is divisive. An employee who disagrees with a poor performance evaluation given by her supervisor exemplifies a conflictive situation. A complex negotiation is one in which there are many issues, but they are not conflictive. This is perhaps the least common category, since the more issues that are at stake, the greater the likelihood some of these will be divisive. Consider, for example, a negotiation involving the renovation of a building that needs structural changes, electrical upgrades, paint-

Figure 22-1. Issues and negotiation complexity.

	Few Issues	Many Issues
Non-Contentious Issues	**Simple**	**Complex**
Contentious Issues	**Conflictive**	**Messy**

ing, furniture, and so on, all within a particular budget. Finally, there are the negotiations that have many issues (indeed, the situation appears to be growing issues), and the issues are divisive. Most public-policy debates fall into this category.

The more parties that are involved in a negotiation, the harder it is to get everyone together and, in general, the more time it takes to reach an agreement. The Uruguay GATT negotiations (General Agreement on Tariffs and Trade), for example, an extremely complex set of negotiations involving over one thousand official delegates from more than seventy countries, took eight years to complete. And the longer negotiations take, the greater the likelihood that new parties will take an interest in the proceedings (making things more complicated) while the interest of existing stakeholders can change in the face of new leadership and shifting priorities. It is also harder to maintain momentum in the press and among constituencies, as sentiment, motivation, and issues all can change over an extended timeframe.

While more issues in a negotiation generally means that the negotiation will be more complicated, introducing additional issues can also mean more opportunities for a creative settlement (for example, when issues that are important to one side but not to the other side, and vice versa, are traded off). When there is a single issue in a negotiation, such as money, the situation is often viewed as a fixed-pie, win-lose proposition. Sometimes it is necessary to create or discover new issues in order to have trade-offs. For example, a labor-management negotiation that initially focuses only on wages might actually be completed more rapidly if the list of issues is expanded to include sick leave and vacation time, which can be traded off against each other.

Similarly, while adding new people to a negotiation may seem like a way of complicating matters, there may be situations where an additional person or two does not complicate and extend the negotiation. On the contrary, this individual may bolster your advantage or decrease your counterpart's leverage. Generally speaking, you want to be the party controlling the addition of new parties and issues to a negotiation.

Given this background, how can you affect leverage to your advantage in a multiparty situation? That is, how can you increase your leverage or decrease the other party's leverage? We begin with a discussion of bilateral negotiations, and then move to more complex multilateral negotiations.

Bilateral Negotiations

To some extent, bilateral negotiations are like many of the two-person negotiations we have already discussed. Only in this case, rather than the negotiation involving you and another person, you are part of a group of individuals or organizations that stands on one side of the issue(s) and there is another group that stands on the other side. Many of the same techniques for altering leverage apply, including matching your products or services to the other side's wants or needs, altering their perceived wants or needs, identifying product or service deficiencies, and feigning other options. However, you are often applying these techniques to multiple individuals.

The task in bilateral negotiations is to keep your side focused and united, while trying to convince spokespeople or key stakeholders on the other side of the relative merits of your position. Ideally, you hope to convince individuals on the other side to become advocates for your position if not to defect to your side.

This challenge is illustrated in a simple game called the Prisoner's Dilemma, which has been used for many years to study human decision making. The game simulates what might happen if two individuals are suspected of committing a crime, but there is not enough evidence to convict either one. The prisoners represent one side, the law enforcement authorities represent the other side. By separating the two prisoners, the authorities can interrogate each prisoner without the other's knowledge. If the prisoners refuse to talk, both will go free; there simply is not enough evidence to convict them. If one agrees to "turn state's evidence" and implicate the other, however, that individual will get a light sentence or freedom, while the other prisoner will serve a long jail term. If both decide to broker a deal with the authorities (each not realizing that the other is talking), then both will serve jail time. The game is called Prisoner's Dilemma because each prisoner is faced with a difficult decision—to talk or not to talk.

With only two prisoners, each prisoner may feel somewhat confident that the other will hold his tongue. But imagine a scenario in which five or ten prisoners are involved. What is the probability that all five or all ten will remain silent? With more prisoners (individuals or groups on the same side), there is a greater probability that one or more will defect to the other side.

The Prisoner's Dilemma has been played out over and over again in the court system. In the Enron scandal, for example, Andrew Fastow agreed to cooperate with authorities in the implication of other executives within the company in return for a lesser sentence for himself and his wife, who was also charged. With multiple executives involved, it was easier for authorities to convince individuals that if they did not cooperate, someone else would. And those who did not cooperate would be treated accordingly.

This type of maneuvering also occurs during federal and state legislative sessions. With a vote that could go either way on an important piece of legislation, a governor will offer certain state representatives funding for their special projects in order to secure their vote. In essence, these individuals are being drawn from one side to another by matching products or services (funding) to their wants or needs (pet projects). If they don't take the special offer, somebody else likely will. The same occurs when promises are made to a key individual whose support is needed to approve a new university governance system, a community bond referendum, or a labor-management agreement.

Alternatively, negotiators have been known to try to break the unity of the other side by turning their members against one another. In the process, the other side's wants and needs change from external (a competition between them and you) to internal (a conflict or negotiation between coalition members). In essence, you try to weaken their cohesiveness or resolve.

Political parties do this in subtle ways, by carefully focusing on issues that are likely to disrupt or divide the opposing party. If they can facilitate a party split, they increase the likelihood that their candidate(s) will be elected. Ross Perot's Reform Party, for example, spun off members of the Republican Party in the 1992 elections in the United States, while Ralph Nader's Green Party did the same to the Democratic Party in the 2000 elections (although it is not clear what impact these third parties ultimately had on presidential election results).

In high-stakes bilateral negotiations, one side may not only try to turn the other side's members against one another, but they may try to place some of their own members inside the other party. These individuals will try to disrupt meetings and tasks in subtle ways, creating internal conflicts that make the group less effective. They also, of course, can gather inside information about the other side's strategy and tactics. The use of spies, informants, agitators, and the like are most common during periods of intense competition and conflict.

The task of keeping your side united in a bilateral negotiation is often easier when there is a small number of individuals involved, and when the costs of defection are greater than the potential gains. Such was the case for the supporting cast of the sitcom "Seinfeld" when they sought to increase their salaries by negotiating as a unit rather than individually. By the eighth season, "Seinfeld" had reached tremendous popularity and the supporting cast of Jason Alexander (George), Julia Louise-Dreyfus (Elaine), and Michael Richards (Kramer) was each making $150,000 per episode. Hoping to take advantage of the series' success, the three asked for a raise to one million dollars per episode. Warren Littlefield, the head of NBC at the time, felt that the network couldn't simply replace the three co-stars with a new set of friends for Jerry. The cast turned down an offer that included stock from the parent company, General Electric, and eventually settled for $600,000 per episode.

The six co-stars of the television show "Friends" followed a similar script, collectively demanding salary increases to $1,050,000 per episode. When the head of NBC's entertainment division, Garth Ancier, offered $700,000, the six actors stood firm in their demand. Despite the fact that "Friends" was the biggest prime-time hit at the time, Ancier asked the promotion department to produce promotional ads saying that the series would end in its eighth season the following Thursday (feigning other options). The cast quickly came back to the negotiating table, although they got their million-dollars-an-episode deal a couple of years later.

The casts of "Seinfeld" and "Friends" undoubtedly learned their lesson in negotiating as a single voice from prior sitcoms. Suzanne Somers was one of three stars of the popular sitcom "Three's Company" back in the 1970s. Making only $5,000 per episode when the series started, and $35,000 five years later when the series had gained popularity, she demanded an increase to $150,000 per episode. Instead, the network wrote her character out of the show. Had she made a pact with the other two members of the show and negotiated as a group, perhaps the outcome would have been different.

Similarly, parents often negotiate as a unit with their children on important issues, executive branches of government try to speak with a single voice, and countries form economic unions that negotiate as a unit. The more incentives there are to remaining united (and the greater the perceived costs of defecting), the more effective a group can be. But it requires significant communication to ensure mutual understanding, trust, and resolve.

You can also strengthen your side's leverage by adding third parties to your side who have special leverage. Consider, for example, the situation involving loud music coming from your neighbor's apartment, sometimes until the wee hours of the morning. You have tried repeatedly to get your neighbor to turn down the music, but the volume only goes back up later in the evening or the next weekend. Other members of your family also are annoyed, along with other people from surrounding apartments. At the same time, there are individuals from the building and elsewhere who sometimes attend your neighbor's late-night events. What can you do?

While you may have little leverage over your neighbor (as the costs of his not complying with your wishes are simply a disgruntled neighbor), his costs are greater if he doesn't comply with the directives of the property manager (a friend of yours). Therefore, you could contact the property manager, explain the situation, and wait for the manager to enforce building rules.

Employing the property manager as an ally to bolster your side's leverage, however, may create negative feelings toward you. It represents an obvious power move. Alternatively, you might be less direct in tapping the influence of a third party. Knowing something about your neighbor and his friends, you could invite someone influential in his life over for dinner on a night when the music is likely to be blaring (such as, someone from the building's executive committee, or from the office where he works). If the guest is equally offended by the noise, there is a good chance she will say something.

These approaches literally involve adding another party to the negotiation. Of course, you could also hint to the neighbor that you have certain friends in high places, which might be enough to reduce his loud behavior. You are, in effect, altering your neighbor's perceived wants or needs—in this case, from playing loud music to remaining on good terms with the building's executive committee—by introducing new costs of not cooperating. If there are multiple stakeholders in his apartment, however, your task becomes more complicated. Each individual may have a different set of wants or needs.

As this example suggests, it helps to have friends in high places (or at least critical places). And it underscores one of the advantages of developing social and professional networks: You increase the chances of making contact with someone who has more leverage than you have. This person can get you an introduction or appointment, recommend your work, support your position, and so on. By putting the names of prominent individuals down as references on your resume, you gain credibility through their reputations and recommendations. Early in my career, I was interested in applying for the executive director's position at a newly created organization. As a freshly minted Ph.D. with minimal experience, I approached a senior individual with a national reputation I had met through a nonprofit organization. We had worked together briefly at this mediation center. I told him that I was interested in applying for the position, but would only do so if he would write a letter of recommendation for me. He agreed, and I became a finalist (although my youth and inexperience were revealed in the interview and I did not get the position).[1]

Using contacts in this way amounts to leveraging leverage. Although you may not have leverage with your counterpart, if you can identify someone with whom you do have leverage, someone who has leverage over your counterpart, you can gain an advantage. Political candidates know this and bring in other political figures, movie personalities, and rock stars to implicitly or explicitly endorse their candidacy with certain voting groups. Advertising firms do the same, employing celebrities to give their products credibility and appeal with different consumer groups.

Sometimes more than one party (lever) is required, which is not without its advantages. The more people (links) there are in the chain, the greater the distance between you (the person seeking to effect the leverage) and the target party. Indeed, there is a principle called "six degrees of separation," which suggests that there are at most six people between any two individuals in the world. You know someone who knows someone who knows someone else who has a friend who is related to the president of General Motors. These connections often are important in effecting leverage, particularly in multiparty negotiations.[2]

Interestingly, while research shows that women are often better than men at networking, their social networks do not always extend to those individuals with legitimate power in an organization (for example, males in executive positions). As a consequence, they may sometimes require longer chains of levers to reach their intended targets, which has its advantages (distance) and potential disadvantages.

The longer the sequence or chain of leveraged parties, however, the more complicated, fragile, and unstable the effort becomes. You are, in fact, creating a leveraging chain in which one weak link can thwart your efforts. In general, one or two links between you and the target party is probably the ideal.[3]

This is not to say, however, that you cannot have multiple distributed levers (for example, multiple references on a resume, multiple celebrities endorsing your candidacy or product). Parties have been known to take explicit and creative steps in this regard to secure the base of their support. Large defense companies in the United States, for example, subcontract with manufacturing plants in key districts throughout the country to ensure the continuation of their projects. The defense company effectively develops a network of constituents (including congressional leaders) who will fight to keep the defense project going for fear of lost jobs. The V-22 Osprey Helicopter serves as an example, a project that failed numerous test performances yet survived in part because its two thousand subcontractors were located in more than forty states.

Similarly, an individual who endears herself to many coworkers makes it more difficult for a supervisor to fire her. Much like the roots of a plant, this individual is entwined with other living matter (in this case, other employees). To attempt to remove her would likely be met by resistance and resentment from other coworkers, some with considerable clout in the organization. Thus, she has implicitly created leverage through extensive networking and relationship building, which translates into potential costs to the supervisor if the firing appears to violate social norms. Multiple distributive levers produce a cumulative effect that can be realized even when some of the levers fail.

Multilateral Negotiations

Multilateral negotiations generally refer to negotiations involving three or more parties with somewhat different or competing interests. As indicated, many public policy negotiations involve this level of complexity. In the worst cases, there are not only many unrelated issues but strong feelings about some of those issues going back many years. The ongoing conflict in the Middle East represents an extreme example.

Negotiations that start out as multilateral sometimes can become bilateral, as the parties align into two camps. The situation in Iraq during the George W. Bush administration, for example, was most probably a multilateral negotiation that became redefined as a bilateral situation (with the United States, Great Britain, and other coalition forces lined up on one side against those countries favoring continued United Nations' inspections).

There is, in fact, some value in reducing the number of distinct parties through coalition formation, assuming your coalition can be held together. With just two parties or sides (a bilateral negotiation), only one negotiation is required (between Party A and Party B). With three parties, there could very likely be three negotiations (A with B, A with C, and B with C). With four sides, the number of potential negotiations jumps to six (A with B, A with C, A with D, B with C, B with D, and C with D); for five parties, the number is ten; and for six parties, there are fifteen potential negotiations required.[4]

It is partly for this reason that the two major political parties in the United States try to limit the emergence of other parties. They do so in a variety of ways, such as through policies and legislation limiting other parties from receiving financial contributions, from participating in televised debates, and from appearing on ballots. They recognize that a third party that draws more-or-less equally from each existing party would make the electoral process more challenging for them.

The more interest groups that are joined in a single coalition, and the more diverse their interests or needs, the harder it is to keep the coalition together. Thus, in a sense the coalition absorbs some of the diversity of an otherwise multilateral negotiation, and the negotiations within the coalition or party become multilateral. The antiwar movement of the 1960s, for example, drew people with diverse agendas, including antiwar activists, civil rights activists, abortion rights activists, feminists, and environmentalists, who were often difficult to keep focused and united.

Generally speaking, you want to include the minimum number of people in a coalition in order to bring about an advantage. For the "Seinfeld" cast, previously mentioned, this meant it was not necessary to include any of the occasional characters (for example, Newman) or even Jerry. Suzanne Somers, however, needed at least one and preferably both of the other central characters in "Three's Company" to join her efforts.

Coalitions can be formed with parties who are adversaries of the other side, friends/allies of the other side, or independents. It seems natural to form coalitions with adversaries of your counterpart, as they are most likely to want to join forces with you. You provide a match for their wants or needs—opposition to the other party. When the United States was seeking its independence from England, for example, France, a long-time adversary of England, helped the colonists in many ways (financial aid, supplies, leadership, troops). The risk of forming a coalition with a counterpart's adversaries, however, is that your counterpart may become more hostile toward you.

You can also try to form a coalition with allies of the other side or with independents. This can be accomplished by increasing the costs to these individuals of not joining your coalition (focusing on their wants and needs, tapping affiliation needs, discrediting or eliminating their alternatives). The danger of forming a coalition with friends or allies of your counterparts is that these individuals may have a change of heart, ultimately turning strategic information over to your counterparts.

Sometimes the best you can hope for is to neutralize the other parties, particularly friends or potential allies of your counterparts, so they do not take sides and enter the fray. As a venerable university dean once put it, the job of a dean is to keep the faculty who hate your guts away from the faculty who are undecided. It is generally in your best interests to be proactive rather than to wait for others to come to you, because in waiting, there is a greater chance of coalitions forming among other stakeholders.[5]

Language can play an important role in attracting individuals to a coalition and in neutralizing others (that is, keeping them from organizing or supporting others). Political leaders will frequently employ engaging language to attract individuals to their cause, or inhibit the organization of opposition. Terms like "tax reform," "health care reform," and "Social Security reform," regardless of what the proposed legislation entails, sound like something that everyone should support. We are all in favor of governmental reform.

Because of the potential diversity of stakeholders and agendas in a multilateral negotiation, leaders will sometimes look for a unifying principle or theme to galvanize various parties. In essence, these leaders are trying to alter the perceived wants or needs of the parties. When Abraham Lincoln became president, for example, it appeared that a civil war in the United States was imminent. He was advised by one of his cabinet members to declare war on a European nation, as a way of altering the perceived wants of Southern states from independence to national unity against a common foe. More recently, Argentine dictator General Leopoldo Galtieri initiated a conflict with Great Britain over the Falkland (Malvinas) Islands, land to which Great Britain had long laid claim even though the islands are just off the coast of southern Argentina. Galtieri's ruling military junta was being threatened by domestic instability, and the act was intended to unify the country in a common goal.

Some years ago, I spearheaded an effort to establish a mediation program as an alternative to small claims court in a county in Wisconsin. We wanted the county to fund the program, of course, which was met by resistance from many county board members. They did not want to see more government programs or any additional government spending. There were many individuals and groups involved in this negotiation, including the county executive, local business leaders, the local bar association, three sitting judges, and local citizens (through news coverage). While we tried many themes and arguments to make our case for a mediation program (such as the time saved by the program, the overall satisfaction of the disputants), we discovered that there was a single argument that worked best. A mediation program would help reduce the growing court backlog, which otherwise would require the county to add a fourth court, costing substantial money to construct and run. We had found an issue that most everyone agreed on. Still, it took three and a half years to build enough support to get the necessary votes.

As you can see from this chapter, multiparty negotiations can be very complicated. Even when all the stakeholders can be accounted for, and often this is not the case when the negotiation commences, there are many different permutations of alliances and coalitions possible, and many different ways of approaching a situation. Turning a multilateral negotiation into a bilateral negotiation through coalition building potentially increases the diversity of the coalition, likely requiring internal multilateral negotiations. In a sense, most department meetings represent multilateral negotiations, with different members bringing their individual items and issues to the meeting's agenda.

Generally speaking, the more complex the negotiation, the more structure and organization you will need to employ in your internal or external meetings and negotiations. Imagine, for example, conducting a negotiation involving a proposed development in your neighborhood, which will impact traffic, existing retail businesses, and property values. You would need more than your memory to keep track of the various representatives, their issues, tentative agreements, and so on. You would want written records. In addition, you would certainly want detailed agendas to structure your meetings, with formal facilitators and notetakers. In a complex and potentially divisive multiparty meeting, you would probably want to follow a formal protocol, such as Robert's Rules of Order, in order to maintain some control.

Table 22-1 lists some guidelines for managing multiparty meetings, including situations where some of the issues are divisive. These guidelines begin with identifying the stakeholders and their issues, perhaps through preliminary, one-on-one negotiations (much like a caucus in a mediation). A plenary meeting of all stakeholders can be managed by limiting the meeting to key spokespersons or representatives rather than entire groups or organizations, establishing formal roles, employing a detailed agenda, and using external memory (notes, handouts, white-boards, etc.) to keep track of information and agreements. Generally, momentum can be built by dealing with noncontentious items first. Throughout deliberations, it is important to remind parties of their collective interests and areas of agreement (the progress being made). The resource section at the end of this book offers several books that you may find useful if you are frequently in a position where you have to manage such meetings.[6]

Finally, to give you an opportunity to practice some of the ideas included in this chapter, a three-party negotiation has been included in Appendix B. This negotiation involves the owners of a sports team who want a new stadium, a property management firm with holdings

Table 22-1. Guidelines for managing messy negotiations.

1. Identify all stakeholders.
2. Identify the issues (including their historical underpinnings).
3. Conduct preliminary negotiations (one-on-one).
4. Hold plenary meetings with key stakeholders and representatives (spokespersons).
5. Structure meetings (specific roles, detailed agendas, round-robin discussions).
6. Employ external memory (handouts, flip-charts, white-boards).
7. Deal with noncontentious issues first to build momentum.
8. Reinforce common interests, areas of agreement.

near the existing stadium, and the government of the county where the current stadium is located. As indicated in the introduction to the negotiation, the simulation can be made still more complicated by turning it into a team-based negotiation.

In completing this negotiation, think about the techniques described in this chapter. During the debriefing, in fact, you may want to assess who had leverage, how it changed, and what techniques were employed to alter leverage. This will begin to give you greater insight into managing complex, multiparty negotiations in the future.

Notes

1. Madeline Albright, who was Secretary of State during the Clinton administration, recognized the special challenges faced by women in traditionally male-dominated roles. As the first female Secretary of State, she had to negotiate with male counterparts around the world. Years later, while on a book tour, she was asked if she ever had any difficulties dealing with Arab men during diplomatic missions. She said that she never had any trouble; she arrived in a big plane with "US of A" on the side. She could hardly have had a more formidable introduction/business card. Her problems, she added, were with American males.

2. Recognizing the value of these chains, a number of social-network services have emerged on the Internet. These services cater to different interest groups, but in effect allow you to work through a network of acquaintances to gain an introduction or interview with an acquaintance of an acquaintance. Two services that focus on building professional relationships through Internet-based networking are Ryze (www.ryze.com) and LinkedIn (www.linkedin.com).

3. As an illustration of the inherent vulnerability of long chains, you might recall an episode from the television sitcom "M*A*S*H" in which Hawkeye desperately needs new boots. The weather is cold and wet, and one of his boots has a sizable hole in the bottom. Frustrated, he goes to the supply officer to demand new boots. His rationalizations and hysterics, however, get him nowhere. Then it is revealed that the supply officer has a tooth problem, which the camp dentist could fix. But the camp dentist has a fascination with Japan, and wants a pass to vacation there before he will touch the tooth. Radar, the company clerk, can find a way to secure the pass, but he wants a date with a

certain nurse in camp. Hawkeye discovers that this nurse would go on a date with anyone if he could get her a hairdryer. Klinger, the company cross-dresser, has a hairdryer but he wants a discharge from the army, which requires the signatures of three officers (which would mean Major Margaret Houlihan or Major Frank Burns, both of whom have refused in the past). Major Houlihan would be willing to sign if Hawkeye and Trapper would treat her paramour Frank Burns better, beginning with a camp birthday party in his honor. But in the middle of the birthday party, one of the levers fails, leading to a domino effect negating the long sequence of agreements.

4. The general formula for determining the number of negotiations required in an n-party negotiation is: $(n^2 - n)/2$.

5. There is a board game called "Diplomacy" that teaches the art of coalition formation. Set in the early twentieth century, the game involves seven players representing European countries. Each player controls armies and fleets, but must forge (and break) alliances with other players in order to survive. The game, which simulates the complexities of Europe before the beginning of World War I, is said to have been a favorite of President John Kennedy and Secretary of State Henry Kissinger. There are also computerized versions of Diplomacy, allowing you to test your skills with players from around the world (for example, check out www.floc.net/dpjudge).

6. It is perhaps worth noting that many of these guidelines apply to mediating a complex dispute, which is another way of thinking about multiparty negotiations. The mediator or meeting facilitator derives advantage through the process itself, whose alternative may well be more unpredictable and costly for the parties. For example, many mediators will use the appeal of the mediation process as leverage to keep one or more of the parties from choosing an adversarial alternative over mediation (for example, by recounting the time, money, and uncertainty of going to court).

23

> You can tell the ideals of a nation by its advertisements.
>
> —Norman Douglas

International Negotiations

With the ever-increasing globalization of world markets, more and more individuals are finding themselves in positions where they must represent their organizations in international negotiations. In some cases, representatives from a foreign company will be traveling to your country for negotiations, while at other times you will be traveling abroad to do business. How does leverage come into play in these situations? What determines who has leverage? And how is this advantage carried out?

Keeping in mind our original axiom (the more it costs the other party not to have an agreement, the more leverage you have), the same principles apply to international negotiations as apply in everyday, domestic negotiations. Consider, for example, the case of an Italian ceramic tile manufacturer that is interested in having its products distributed by a large U.S. retail chain, by far the largest retail chain of its type in the country. As the Italian tiles are of high quality, they are most likely to be sold in an upscale market. The United States represents one of the best such markets, which is already served by several quality tile manufacturers. Given these conditions, who appears to have leverage in this situation? And what are the implications of this advantage?

Because the costs of no agreement appear to be greater for the Italian manufacturer than the U.S. retail distributor, the advantage would be with the U.S. distributor. The Italian manufacturer wants the

U.S. distributor, because they serve a large market with the greatest potential for their products (Question #1, "What do I want?"). Because they are by far the largest of all U.S. distributors, no other single distributor will substitute for this company (Question #3, "What are my alternatives?"). At the same time, the U.S. distributor has other options since there are several quality tile manufacturers.

What if the case hadn't specified, however, the size of the U.S. retail chain or that this chain was already being served by several quality tile manufacturers? Are there other, more generic factors related to the two countries in this scenario—Italy and the United States—that would give us a clue as to who is likely to have leverage? What broad factors in an international negotiation suggest wants/needs and alternatives, the bases of leverage?

There are at least seven country factors worth considering before undertaking an international negotiation: natural resources, geography, history, technology/labor force, economy/legal system, consumer base, and culture. Each of these factors can influence leverage in the broadest context, and each should be analyzed for all countries represented in a negotiation.

Natural Resources

Natural resources often can provide a clue as to who has leverage in international negotiations. There are some countries, for example, that have advantages in certain areas (such as, oil, gas, fresh water, arable land) that other countries naturally desire. Saudi Arabia, for example, is the world's largest oil producer. Australia produces most of the world's aluminum. Canada supplies most of the world's potash, a form of fertilizer. On the other hand, Japan has few natural resources and must import most of its minerals, energy, and food products.

Some natural resources are clearly more essential than others. Oil and gas, for example, are heating and manufacturing necessities for the industrialized West. South Africa, on the other hand, is known for its diamonds and gold. Although valued in many contexts, diamonds do not share the same life-essential quality that oil and water possess. And gold, while essential in the manufacture of jewelry, watches, computer technology, medical equipment, and much more, is more valuable in these transformed states than as a raw material. Even some food products (wheat and rice) appear to be more critical to people's health and welfare than do other foods (caviar).

While many natural resources have an enduring quality, most will not last forever. As some countries have depleted their own natural resources, those of other regions have become more valuable. The Amazon rain forests of Brazil, for example, have become so precious in terms of rare species of plants and animals as well as protection of the earth's atmosphere through carbon dioxide absorption that there has been serious talk of swapping some of Brazil's international debt for rainforest preservation.

Nonetheless, resources can be discovered or developed elsewhere, which can change a country's perceived relative advantage. In Equatorial Guinea, for example, a large oil field was discovered in 1995, changing the economy and politics of that country dramatically. The development of synthetic rubber in the 1940s changed the demand for natural rubber from Southeast Asia. In recent years, some countries have begun farming salmon and other seafood, which has changed the dynamics of the fishing industry. Thus, understanding a country's natural resource advantages and deficiencies can provide insight as to who has leverage and in what contexts.

Geography

Geography is another factor that can give a country an advantage. Geography, of course, is associated with natural resources. As noted, Saudi Arabia is rich in oil. Argentina has topsoil and grasslands that are perfect for raising cattle. The Netherlands' climate is ideal for growing tulips. These geographic factors give them specific advantages that other countries may not have.

Geography is also important in terms of access to waterways (an economical way of transporting goods), national defense, and historical identity. Iraq, for example, has little in the way of deep-water access to the Persian Gulf and, ultimately, the Indian Ocean. Its access is blocked by Kuwait. The Iraqi invasion of Kuwait in 1990 was motivated, at least in part, by a desire to gain more direct access to the sea. (It also was motivated by the Iraqi claim that Kuwait was slant-drilling across its border to tap into an Iraqi oil field.) Likewise, the Suez Canal in Egypt represents an important waterway connecting Europe with Asia.

Many of the world's most powerful nations have been giving up control of strategic lands only recently and somewhat reluctantly, while holding onto others. The United States, for example, started transferring control of the Panama Canal to Panama in the 1970s, a transfer that was completed in 1999. The United States, however, maintains military bases in countries throughout the world, including Germany, Saudi Arabia, Guam, Iceland, Italy, Spain, Japan, Korea, Cuba, Diego Garcia, and Bahrain. Hawaii's strategic location is one of the reasons it is the fiftieth state in the United States.

Having military bases in these strategic locations helps a country protect its interests locally as well as throughout the region. When the September 11th World Trade Center attack was traced to Al Qaeda forces in Afghanistan, Pakistan's geographic proximity to Afghanistan gave it leverage with the U.S. military looking to reduce sanctuary for Osama bin Laden and to invade Afghanistan.

President Kennedy's program in the 1960s, Alliance for Progress, was a response to the Communist threat that began in Cuba. Fearing that other Caribbean, Central American, or South American countries could move politically toward the former Soviet Union, Kennedy sought to increase understanding and improve relations between the north and south. When the Berlin Wall fell and the Soviet threat diminished, however, the United States began to show less and less interest in the region.

Generally speaking, geography is slow to change, and the primary large-scale threats to the earth's geography derive from human actions (global warming, nuclear catastrophe). And while space exploration represents the twenty-first century equivalent of the fifteenth century's exploration and colonization of the New World, space exploration does not constititute an immediate opportunity. Therefore, a country's geography represents distinct advantages and disadvantages in a negotiation.

History

There are, of course, historical reasons behind how geopolitical maps are drawn, a history that can provide valuable information about the ideals and necessities of a country. Many of the world's international conflicts are based on hundreds if not thousands of years of habitation and tradition, which must be understood to effectively negotiate peace. The Jewish and Arab claims on Jerusalem, for example, go back thousands of years. There are certain areas in Jerusalem, such as Temple Mount, which both cultures believe to be holy sites, albeit for different reasons. The former Soviet Union's invasion of Eastern Europe and the subsequent formation of the Communist Bloc following World War II was an effort to create a buffer between Moscow and the rest of Europe, given the lessons of Hitler's invasion of the Soviet Union in 1941 and Napoleon's designs on the region 130 years earlier.

Many countries have developed strong affiliations and alliances, which can influence leverage in negotiations. These affiliations are sometimes based on similarities in language and custom (religion), but might just as likely be tied to events in their history. A Dutch friend told me the story of a colleague from Canada visiting his country for an extended period. The two went out to buy a car, which the Canadian negotiated. Before the contract was signed, however, the Dutch friend asked for his turn at negotiating with the car salesman. Arguing strongly that Canada had sent troops to help free The Netherlands from German occupation during World War II, at the loss of many lives, he was able to get the price lowered still further. The historical contributions were undeniable . . . and leveragable.

The history of a country often is embodied in the organization of cities, its monuments and artifacts from antiquity (the Parthenon in Greece, the pyramids of Egypt), foods, language, and entertainment (sports). All of these factors, along with economic and political considerations, go into determining which cities will be selected to host international events. The choice of Athens to host the 2004 Summer Olympics, for example, was undoubtedly influenced by the fact that the 26-mile marathon was named for an important event in Greek history and the first modern Olympics were held there in 1896.

History also can provide valuable information regarding uncertainty and risk associated with a country. A country that has experienced periods of political unrest, for example, offers a different negotiating challenge/opportunity than a country that is seen as stable and predictable (Switzerland, for example). This type of information can affect the projection of what one wants in a negotiation (demand), and how badly one wants it.

Technology/Labor Force

There are also technological advantages that certain countries possess that can directly affect leverage, including computer hardware and software development, automobile manufacture, defense systems, pharmaceuticals, and so on. A negotiator whose country's products are more advanced and desirable will naturally have an advantage in a negotiation.

To illustrate, some years ago, when computer speed and capacity were improving dramatically every year or two, a good friend was in the market for a new personal computer. She decided to sell her outdated IBM computer through a local newspaper. While she had almost no interested buyers, one inquiry finally came from a man from the former Soviet Union. He stopped by with another man to look at the machine, asked a few questions, and eventually bought it for one or two hundred dollars.

At the time, the purchase seemed peculiar to her, because this machine was clearly out of date and soon to be obsolete. Why did he buy it? One possible explanation is that the former Soviet Union was well behind most Western nations in terms of this technology. They needed something, anything, that would close the technology gap. In other words, my friend had something they badly needed.

A number of countries have emerged as leaders in various areas of technology. Japan is known as a leader in robotics, among other areas. India has developed a reputation for software programming. Switzerland is well known for its banking and financial systems. The United States is a leader in the development of medical technology.

These technologies are a function of the skill level of the workforce, which is often reinforced by government efforts to support, promote, and expand that advantage. Skill level, however, need not be highly sophisticated to be valuable to a technology. China's emerging power in world commerce is based as much on the size of its workforce (and the fact that it is a relatively inexpensive workforce, by Western standards) as on its unique expertise.

Technological differences can change more rapidly than natural resource advantages. The United States' advantage over Japanese automakers evaporated in the decades following World War II. The technological gap between the West and countries from the former Soviet Union began to narrow after the Berlin Wall came down and many of the newly formed countries moved to a free-market system. South Africa is training its workforce to craft many of the products that contain its gold, rather than exporting this raw material to other countries for manufacturing purposes.

International Negotiations

Understanding technological advantages, and where changes are occurring, can be valuable in international negotiations. The more central an emerging technology is to the sustenance and development of the rest of the world, and the fewer countries that can produce that new technology, the more leverage a country on the cutting edge will have.

Economy/Legal System

In addition, the economic conditions of a country can suggest an advantage or disadvantage in negotiations. In many cases, the economy of a country is linked to one or more of the factors already profiled (geography, natural resources, technology). As noted, Japanese technological superiority began to emerge in the years following World War II, and the country experienced an "economic miracle" in the 1980s. Awash in capital, Japan sought to diversify. A healthy portion of that money was invested in real estate (high-priced hotels, office buildings, condominiums, golf courses), particularly in the United States.

Knowing that a country is cash rich or cash poor can influence when and how one proceeds with a negotiation. It's like asking your boss for a raise. Do you approach her after the company has just reported record profits or a record loss? What is a country's financial situation? What debt are they carrying?

Economic conditions can affect currency rates as well. More than one organization has ended up on the short end of a deal because it failed to understand currency fluctuations and exchange rates. They negotiated a contract in the unstable currency of another country and, as a consequence, ended up receiving far less payment than expected when the contract was consummated.

Similarly, the legal system of a country can serve as a form of leverage in a negotiation. Contracts can explicitly state which country's legal system (tariffs, import-export laws) will take precedence if there is a dispute, or this may be implied in the contract. In some cases, a contract will refer to other documents that may stipulate a different legal system.

On a broader scale, countries engage in legal agreements to stimulate productivity and trade. In 1994, the United States, Canada, and Mexico signed the North American Free Trade Agreement (NAFTA), which was designed to create a free trade zone between these countries. Other regions of the world have created similar partnerships (MERCOSUR, in South America; CARICOM, in the Caribbean; and the European Union). To the extent that these agreements reduce the number of alternatives available to a company seeking a favorable deal, they influence leverage in a negotiation.

Consumer Base

Nearly all of the trading partners of the United States are afforded what is called Normal Trade Relations (NTR), formerly known as Most Favored Nation status. As a consequence, the same tariffs apply to each of these countries when products enter the United States.[1] However, there are some additional countries that must obtain an annual presidential waiver to continue their NTR status. One of these countries is China. In recent years, China's NTR status has been challenged in some quarters on the basis of its human rights record. Still, this preferred status has been extended year after year. If there are significant human rights violations, why is this status continually renewed? Why is China afforded this status while Cuba, another Communist country, is not?

There are many reasons for this continuance, not the least of which is the fact that China has the largest population in the world. The Chinese economy has shown tremendous growth potential, as many industrialized nations have turned to this relatively inexpensive labor force for manufacturing. If you look carefully, you will see "Made in China" on everything from clothes to water scooters. But China also represents a huge consumer market. As their economy continues to strengthen, their population becomes one of the prime markets for more and more goods. This is a consumer market that Western nations cannot ignore. Thus, there is leverage in a country's consumer base.

The greatest leverage, of course, would come from a consumer base that is not only large, but also affluent (which relates to the country's economy) and isolated or deprived (which relates to the country's political history). Such a country would demand not only tremendous quantities of goods and services, but also expensive items. There is probably not one country that fits this profile. The populations of China and India are by far the largest, followed by the United States, Indonesia, Brazil, Pakistan, and Russia. The United States is the most affluent of these countries. Following the fall of the Berlin Wall and the dissolution of the Soviet Union, many Western countries were eager to take advantage of Russian markets that had been tightly controlled for many years.

As these and previous examples suggest, consumer bases can change. Markets can be opened to deprived consumers, as was the case for the former Soviet Union and other Communist Bloc countries in the 1980s. Countries can experience profit windfalls, which make them more desirable, such as in the case of Japan in the 1970s and 1980s. Countries can even experience dramatic increases in their consumer base through trade agreements and alliances with other countries. Each can increase their leverage in the global marketplace.

Culture

Recall in an earlier chapter that we talked about the different ways that leverage might be signaled between parties. Among the indicators were which party had initiated the negotiation and the meeting location. Given that the U.S. distributor in the example presented at the beginning of this chapter probably had leverage over the Italian tile manufacturer, we might expect representatives from the Italian manufacturer to travel to the United States to make their case. (If the opposite occurs, it suggests that the U.S. distributor may have its own special needs, which it perceives the Italian manufacturer can satisfy. Thus, the manufacturer has some leverage.)

While the travel indicator probably rings true in most countries around the world, there are other indicators that are country or region specific. That is, a behavior that might signal leverage in North America could simply reflect an everyday practice or tradition in another country. Consider, for example, the titles/positions of the representatives. What if the Italian tile manufacturer sent its president rather than the head of the marketing department? Would this signal leverage to the Americans? What if the company was from Japan? Germany? Brazil? Hierarchy plays an important role in many countries in determining who represents the organization in a negotiation. In many Latin American countries, for example, it is often the individual at the top of the hierarchy who will conduct negotiations. Thus, a visit by the president of a Brazilian company may not be a signal that the other party has leverage.

I experienced this some years ago when I became the president of a nonprofit, volunteer organization called DC Partners of Brasilia. DC Partners is a member of Partners of the Americas (an offshoot of Kennedy's Alliance for Progress), which pairs up states in the United States with countries and regions in Central America, South America, and the Caribbean. The purpose of these pairings is to develop better understanding and relations between the two hemispheres through social exchanges and joint projects involving the arts, health care, sports, the environment, and so on. DC Partners of Brasilia pairs the capitals of the United States (Washington, D.C.) and Brazil (Brasilia). Despite the fact that DC Partners had two vice presidents and several project managers, individuals in comparable positions in Brasilia always wanted to deal with me, the president. At the same time, Brasilia's president represented their organization in all functions and negotiations.[2] The lofty organizational position of an individual negotiating on behalf of a Latin American organization does not necessarily signal a lack of leverage; this practice is part of Latin American tradition.

In contrast, in many Asian countries, the decision-making process is collective and consensual. Consequently, a team of negotiators (a lead negotiator with confederates) is likely to represent a Chinese company's concerns, not a single negotiator. The presence of confederates in this case does not necessarily signal a negotiating advantage; it is part of the custom related to how decisions are made throughout much of the Orient.

Several other indicators from Table 5-1 take on a different meaning when viewed through a cultural lens. For example, the lack of eye contact or interruptions on the part of a Japanese negotiator does not necessarily signal that the other party has leverage. Rather, the maintenance of face and honor for all involved parties is essential in Japanese culture, which is affected by limiting both eye contact and interruptions, particularly in tense or controversial situations.

Similarly, Japanese negotiators might be inclined to speak less than negotiators from some Latin American or Middle Eastern countries. This does not necessarily mean they have less leverage in a negotiation. It may be easy for someone from Brazil, however, who is not familiar with Japanese customs, to assume an advantage.

In many parts of the world, gift giving is almost as natural as shaking hands in the United States. A business representative in India, for example, would customarily bring gifts for his negotiating counterpart and possibly family members, depending on how well the principals know one another. This does not necessarily suggest that the U.S. representative has leverage, although he might interpret it that way. It is simply a tradition in Asia and Latin America, the Middle East, and Africa to bring gifts when meeting potential business partners.

In addition, many countries have different orientations toward time and space than are customarily found in North America. Meetings in Latin America, for example, almost always start late. This does not mean that Latin American negotiators always have a perceived advantage, because they show up late for a meeting. Again, it is simply part of the Latin American custom. (Not showing up at all, however, might signal a perceived advantage.)

Also, there is a different appreciation for space in Latin America and the Middle East. In these regions, people stand closer and there is more touching, including hugging and kissing. It does not necessarily mean, however, that the party doing the most touching has a negotiating advantage.

Consequently, you need to understand the culture of a country in order to be able to interpret the indicators of leverage. It may be somewhat more complicated than illustrated in Table 5-1, which profiles Western indicators, but there are nonetheless culturally based indicators that can be used to your advantage. These indicators may include demographic factors—such as the age and gender of negotiators—as well as specific behaviors.

Even the negotiator role, mediated by culture, can signal advantage. Consider, for example, a buyer-seller negotiation in Japan. It is the custom in most such negotiations for the buyer to automatically be afforded leverage in Japan. "The buyer is kinger," as the expression goes. This means that the seller defers to the buyer's wishes and judgment. In effect, the seller trusts the buyer to treat him fairly.

All this is to suggest that it may be possible to profile countries or regions of the world based on their wants or needs as well as their alternatives by looking at one or more broad factors—natural resources, geography, history, technology/labor force, economy/legal system, consumer base, and culture. To do so allows one to recognize his or her advantage in an international negotiation generally, although company or negotiator-specific information also should be sought.

There are a number of sources of information on these factors, including articles and books written on specific countries. Table 23-1 offers some Internet-based resources where information on these seven factors can be found. Depending on how important an interna-

Table 23-1. Sources of information on country characteristics.

Web Site	Countries	Natural Resources	Geography	History	Technology/ Labor	Economy/ Legal	Consumers	Culture
www.cia.gov/cia/publications/factbook (Guide to Country Profiles)	All	X	X		X	X	X	
www.countrystudies.us	Most Countries	X	X	X	X	X		
www.state.gov (Countries and Regions/ Background Notes)	All Except U.S.	X	X	X	X	X	X	
www.wikipedia.com	All	X	X	X	X	X	X	X
www.usaid.gov (Country Locator)	Developing Countries				X	X	X	
www.worldbank.org (Countries & Regions)	Developing Countries				X	X	X	
www.executiveplanet.com	All							X

tional negotiation is to you or your company, and how new you are to negotiating in that region, you may also want to consult some additional sources as well as consider employing an agent with experience in the target country.

Notes

1. In recent years, Cuba and North Korea have been excluded from Normal Trade Relations. Several other countries, such as Iran, Iraq, and Libya, have NTR but the U.S. has imposed trade embargoes on those countries.

2. This is most likely due to the importance of relationships in negotiating in Latin America, the informality of many agreements (more symbolic than formal, more general than specific), and the questionable effectiveness of their legal systems. By developing a strong relationship with the head of an organization, one knows that there is always a friend with the authority to handle any contractual uncertainties or surprises that might arise.

24

> The manner of giving is worth more than the gift.
>
> —Pierre Corneille

Surrendering Leverage

When my godson was going through his formative years, I had the opportunity to teach him how to ride a bike, shuffle a deck of cards, and play golf. We also played checkers and chess. At a young age he had not yet caught on to all the nuances of these board games. He often did not see the potential for double and triple jumps in checkers, for example. At the same time, he did not like to lose. So, if I executed a double jump, he became upset and wanted to take back the move he had made that made my double jump possible.

In the game of checkers, I had an advantage. I had played the game many times, and was better versed in the subtleties of play. Eventually, I recognized that if I was going to be able to teach him how to play this game, I was going to have to give up some of my advantage.

There are negotiating situations where "giving up" leverage may be to your advantage. If the outcome of the negotiation is not that important in the grand scheme of life, as was the case in those games of checkers, you may not want to reveal, let alone press, your advantage. There are a variety of reasons why this may be the case: the other party's low self-esteem, the tenuous nature of the relationship, the relatively low importance of the issue's outcome, etc.

There are several ways in which leverage can be "surrendered." One way is to simply obscure it. Recall that leverage is based on perceptions. If the other party does not perceive that he or she is at a disadvantage, then the most that can exist is Potential leverage. By not taking action to bring the disadvantage to light, you in effect obscure or hide your leverage.

This frequently occurs between countries where, through a network of intelligence-gathering agents, information about the questionable or illegal activities of the other country's leaders is acquired. To share such information could jeopardize the friendly relations between the two countries. Consequently, it is Potential leverage that is not activated.

When I was growing up, young women would often obscure their advantage over the young men they were interested in. Recognizing that the social play of boys and men is often about status, these women would pretend not to be as strong or as smart as the young men whose interest they sought to capture. In some cases, they would exaggerate this to the point of feigning helplessness. In so doing, the egos of the young men were kept intact if not inflated, and the women were able to get the men's attention. This social phenomenon is aptly depicted in the musical *Annie Get Your Gun*, in which Annie Oakley falls in love with the shooting ace of a Wild West show, Frank Butler. Annie is a better shooter than Frank, and perhaps is at least his equal in a number of other events, as the song "Anything You Can Do, I Can Do Better" sung by Annie suggests. But this approach embarrasses Frank, and only makes Annie's quest more difficult, as symbolized by the song "You Can't Get a Man With a Gun."

Another way of surrendering leverage is to deactivate it. If, perchance, Potential leverage becomes Active leverage, you can seek to deactivate it by suggesting that you are unaware of the advantage or that the advantage is not real or important. For example, a diplomat from the observed country hints that some leaders of his county may be involved in inappropriate activities. His counterpart could simply play dumb, suggesting that she does not know what he is talking about. This defuses the advantage before it is fully activated. If the diplomat from the observed country were to reveal this information, his counterpart could deactivate the leverage by denying the authenticity of the information.

Still another approach is to offer some advantage to the other party as a way of balancing leverage. In the international scenario presented above, the counterpart might respond to hints that leaders in the observed country are involved in illegal activities by suggesting that the leaders of all countries are probably involved in some sort of shady

Surrendering Leverage

dealings, including the leader of her own country: It is the nature of politics. Thus, by suggesting that each side is at a disadvantage, the leverage becomes balanced.

To some extent, this was the basis for the policy of Mutual Assured Destruction (MAD), which governed U.S.–Soviet foreign relations following World War II. Each country had enough nuclear weapons to destroy the other country many times over, without defense. If one country were to take preemptive action, the other country would respond immediately. Both countries would be annihilated. Thus, such a preemptive act was in effect suicide.

Although this policy seemed to have had its intended effect, at least as of this writing, sometimes mutual leverage escalates out of control. During an episode of the sitcom "Friends," Ross and Monica (brother and sister) lose control and begin revealing embarrassing information that each has about the other in the company of their parents. Monica reveals the truth regarding who was actually smoking pot years ago when their father detected it—Ross, not Chandler—as a means of changing her parents' feelings toward Chandler, her boyfriend. She then adds that it was Ross stealing dad's *Playboy* magazines years ago, not the mailman dad got fired. Ross reveals that it was Monica who broke the family porch swing years ago, not a hurricane, and Monica counters that Ross hasn't worked at the museum for a year. Ross then reveals that Monica and Chandler are living together, and Monica responds that Ross married Rachel in Las Vegas and got divorced . . . again.

Surrendering leverage, of course, can be taken as a sign of weakness by the other party, and used to the other party's advantage. Offering the other party information about your weak negotiating position (desperation for a particular product or for a sale) can give them an advantage you did not intend. If there is an existing relationship between the two of you (or a potential relationship), this is generally a good situation in which to surrender leverage. If you have other Potential leverage, then surrendering some but not all of your leverage can signal your intent to cooperate rather than to compete.

You might also consider the manner in which the leverage is surrendered. In complex, divisive negotiations, a third party can sometimes be useful. For example, a mediator, in private meetings or caucuses with each party to a dispute, can sometimes float proposals as his or her idea rather than the idea of one of the parties, which can be denied or retracted by the other party.

25

> A wise man will make more
> opportunities than he finds.
>
> —Francis Bacon

Final Thoughts

Ted Leonsis is a successful businessman who made his fortune as an Internet pioneer (most notably, with America Online). In 1999, he became a minority owner of the Washington Wizards professional basketball team. After Michael Jordan had left the Chicago Bulls, the Wizards were interested in having him join their organization as president of basketball operations. Leonsis met with Jordan to discuss the possibility, his first meeting ever with the basketball icon. Despite his success in business, Leonsis was nervous in this meeting, and finally communicated his discomfort to Michael Jordan. What does Michael Jordan do when he finds himself in a tense situation, such as the closing moments of an important game, Leonsis asked? Trust your instincts, was Jordan's reply, instincts that are honed through hours of practice.

Like playing basketball, negotiating is skill-based. Therefore, just as you can improve your crossover dribble or your free-throw shooting through practice, you also can improve your negotiating skills through repetition. There are plenty of opportunities to do so in everyday life. Take advantage of these situations. The more you practice the techniques and lessons for managing leverage, the better you will get.

Don't simply wait for a situation to present itself, however. As suggested by an earlier quote, leverage is a bit like gravity: Both are all around us, and so familiar to us, we do not always recognize the central role they play in our lives. During encounters with friends, colleagues, salespeople, and others, you are affected by a perceived negotiating advantage or disadvantage, without necessarily attributing that imbalance to something tangible. Yet it is there, affecting your attitude and behavior.

So rather than waiting for gravity to tap you on the shoulder, think about creating some opportunities for practicing these new negotiating techniques. Think about all the implicit and explicit contracts you currently have, such as for your home or apartment (electricity, natural gas, cable television, property insurance, lawn care, and so on). Which of these might you renegotiate? Think about the purchases you will likely make this week. Which techniques might you practice with these?

In doing so, keep in mind what constitutes a good negotiation. A successful negotiation is one where you get what you want, and the other party feels good enough about the encounter that he or she wants to negotiate with you in the future. If you can succeed in this, life will be full of opportunities and promise.

Resources

Alinsky, S.D. *Rules for Radicals: A Practical Primer for Realistic Radicals*. New York: Vintage, 1989.
Babcock, L., and S. Laschever. *Women Don't Ask: Negotiation and the Gender Divide*. Princeton, N.J.: Princeton University Press, 2003.
Greene, R. *The 48 Laws of Power*. New York: Penguin Books, 2000.
Negotiating (video). Watertown, Mass.: American Management Association Video, 1993.
Robert, H.M. *Robert's Rules of Order* (10th ed.). Reading, Mass.: Perseus, 2000.
Shell, G.R. *Bargaining for Advantage: Negotiation Strategies for Reasonable People*. New York: Viking, 1999.
Streibel, B.J. *The Manager's Guide to Effective Meetings*. New York: McGraw-Hill, 2003.
Tannen, D. *You Just Don't Understand: Women and Men in Conversation*. New York: Ballantine, 1990.
Volkema, R.J. *The Negotiation Toolkit: How to Get Exactly What You Want in Any Business or Personal Situation*. New York: AMACOM, 1999.
Zartman, I.W., and J.Z. Rubin. *Power and Negotiation*. Ann Arbor, Mich.: University of Michigan Press, 2000.

Appendix A: Mafia (An Intriguing and Useful Parlor Game)

"Mafia" is a parlor game that involves all facets of human communication—verbal and nonverbal, public and private—in an attempt to gain control of a community. It is ideally played with 10–12 people, and can be played in several different ways and often repeatedly during the course of a gathering. In most versions of the game there are four roles: a Moderator, Mafia members, Citizens, and a Detective (who is also a Citizen). One person in the group agrees to be the Moderator, who regulates the game. Everyone else is either a Citizen or a member of the Mafia. In a game of 10 to 12 people, three individuals would be members of the Mafia. The Moderator will designate Mafia members by asking everyone to put his or her head down and passing by everyone, touching those chosen to be Mafia on the head. The Moderator would do the same for the Detective, by passing a second time and touching him or her on the head or shoulder.

The game is played over a series of "days" and "nights," nighttime occurring when everyone but the Moderator closes their eyes and puts their head down. During the day, everyone is awake and discusses whom to "kill." It takes a majority vote to kill someone. The objective of the Citizens is to kill off (eliminate) all the Mafia members over a series of days. Meanwhile, members of the Mafia are pretending to be Citizens during the day, but also killing a Citizen every night. The Mafia's goal is to become a majority of the remaining players, because then the Citizens can no longer vote by majority to eliminate a Mafia member, and the Mafia are mathematically the winners.

People are eliminated during the day by a simple vote. Someone lodges a formal accusation against another person, and that person has a chance to defend him- or herself. (Of course Mafia members are likely to accuse non-Mafia members of being Mafia.) There is lots of discussion, innuendos, finger-pointing, logical arguments, bluffing, and so on. There are even private conversations. Finally, the Moderator asks for a vote regarding the accused and counts raised hands. If a majority vote is obtained, that individual is then eliminated. Eliminated or "dead" people may remain to observe the game, much like the Moderator, but may not talk or communicate with the living. Those eliminated also can leave the room until the game is over. At most one person can be eliminated per day, but there can be multiple accusations. When there is no more activity, the Moderator tells everyone it is now nighttime and to go to sleep. Everyone shuts their eyes and puts their heads down.

At night the Mafia acts secretly. All the players have their heads down and eyes closed at night so no one can see who is doing the killing. Only the Moderator knows who is Mafia and they communicate during the night with nonverbal signals that the Moderator watches for. For example, the Moderator would ask "Do you want to eliminate _____?," and waits for a signal. The Moderator asks each person's name every night. When night is over, the Moderator announces who if anyone is dead.

The first night is a special night, however. On the first night the Moderator tells the Mafia to wake up and choose their victims. This is called a "grace night" and is for planning purposes. During this night, while Citizens have their heads down, the Mafia members look up to see who belongs to the Mafia and they signal to one another who they want to eliminate first, second, and third (over the next three nights). They are not locked into this sequence, but it is a plan. The subsequent three nights the Mafia members operate blind (heads down, eyes closed). A simple majority of Mafia votes is required to eliminate someone during the night. So if there are three Mafia members and one abstains and the other two vote for different people, no one dies. But if all the Mafia abstain save one, that is a majority of votes. There is

Appendix A: Mafia (An Intriguing and Useful Parlor Game)

another grace night after three nights of eliminating Citizens to allow for more Mafia planning.

One of the citizens is a Detective. This is a special role in that every night the Detective wakes at the time designated by the Moderator and points at a person to check. The Moderator will indicate by a head nod or shake if that person is in the Mafia. This is the only factual way to determine Mafia members. All other methods are conjecture. The Detective generally wants to hide his identity until he has useful information, because the Mafia will eliminate the Detective to protect themselves.

One variation of this game includes another role, that of a Sniper. The Sniper gets to eliminate one person during one night of the game (a one-shot assassination, with no votes). This variation makes the numbers and roles more difficult to keep track of when trying to devise a hypothesis about what happened and what will happen. The Moderator announces each person's name while all heads are down and eyes closed, just as with the Mafia. If the Sniper wants to eliminate someone, he or she will signal when the name is called.

All in all, the game provides fascinating intrigue while testing one's ability to detect bluffs and lies, to reason, and to communicate (particularly persuasion). If played several times during a given gathering, people will often begin to notice patterns in the behavior of their friends that suggest honesty, deceit, and roles.

Appendix B: Three-Party Negotiation

This negotiation involves three parties—the owners of a sports team (who are interested in building a new stadium for their team), a property management company (which owns property adjacent to the existing stadium), and a county government (which owns the stadium where the team currently plays). This is a fairly complex negotiation, not just because it involves three parties rather than two, but because the issues are not all clearly delineated and there is not a definitive or ideal solution/agreement that is possible.

If you want to make this negotiation still more challenging, you can turn it into a team-based negotiation. Each of the three parties is represented by a team of 3 to 5 people. Thus, you will need to manage the negotiations within your team as well as those between teams. Should you decide to go this route, be sure to allot more time for the simulation. To add still another twist, I have occasionally run this negotiation with individuals or teams communicating entirely over the Internet using e-mail messages. Depending on people's schedules, you may need two or three weeks for this version.

Regardless of which level of complexity you choose, be sure to review the concepts and techniques on leverage before engaging the other party(ies). And when the negotiation is completed, be sure to debrief the exercise (that is, have an open discussion of strategies and techniques employed, and assess what you would do the same and differently next time).

The confidential information for each of the three roles follows.

Alpha Sports Group
Confidential Information

You are a member of a limited partnership that owns a national football team. Your group purchased the team seven years ago for what was at the time the most ever paid for a sports team. During the first few years of ownership, the team (called the Cobras) did well and attendance was near capacity. However, more recently attendance has suffered. This is due to the mediocre performance of the team following the retirement of its popular and brilliant head coach, and to the competition for fans and patrons from two other sports in the metropolitan area as well as a major amusement park.

The revenue-generating potential for the team is limited by the size and design of the current stadium, which was built twenty-five years ago. The current stadium has the smallest seating capacity of any stadium in the league. Furthermore, it lacks the expensive luxury suites that many of the newer stadiums enjoy. These luxury suites are generally purchased by major corporations, and they can command as much as $100,000 each per season. There are two stadiums currently under construction by other teams in the league that will have one hundred eighty of these luxury suites.

Your group would like to build a new stadium with an increased capacity (from the current 50,000 seats to 80,000 seats) and with 180 to 200 luxury suites. Cala County owns the current stadium and parking. You currently pay Cala Country $10 million per year to lease the stadium, which they maintain. Your lease with Cala County expires in three years, so the timing is good to negotiate a deal for land and development assistance.

Two scenarios are possible. The first (and preferred option) is to share the costs and revenues for the new stadium with county government. Under this scenario, your group would put up 30 to 40 percent of the money to build the stadium and county government would provide the remainder. In addition, the county and city governments would provide and maintain the infrastructure for the stadium (roads, sewers, etc.). There are several possibilities for revenue sharing, including for the county to receive a percentage of ticket sales, a percentage of parking revenues, a percentage of concessions (food, beverage), or some combination of these. The average ticket price will probably be around $75, the average parking fee $15 per person, and the average concession intake per customer around $10.

Appendix B: Three-Party Negotiation

The second scenario is for your group to build the stadium with your own money and additional money from private investors. Under this option, county and city governments would still provide roads, sewers, etc. The benefits to the public sector would be job creation and tax revenue. This second scenario is less appealing to your group because of the need for additional investors. The new stadium would cost at least $180 million to build. The profit from all sales (tickets, parking, food, and so on) is about 8 percent of gross.

Two primary locations are being considered for the new stadium. One location is in Cala County, in the large city block next to the current stadium. Once completed, the current stadium could be demolished and more parking added. The second location is ten miles away in an adjacent state that does not have a stadium or a team. While your group has some desire to remain in the current location, your loyalty is not such that you would pay any price to remain.

Given your preferences for location and government participation, there are two primary negotiations that must be completed. One is a negotiation with the owners of the land adjacent to the current stadium. This land is owned by a property management company (Falcon Properties, Inc.), and is presently occupied by a variety of souvenir shops, bars, and restaurants. You estimate the value of this piece of land to be about $18 million. The second negotiation will be with Cala County government officials (who, in turn, will represent city interests).

Falcon Properties, Inc.
Confidential Information

You represent a property management company called Falcon Properties, Inc. (FPI). FPI is one of the largest property management companies in the metropolitan area, owning and managing more than 200 properties. Among those properties are five large apartment complexes and two shopping malls.

One of the properties that FPI owns and manages is a three city-block area of commercial space next to a football stadium. This area contains primarily boutiques, bars, and restaurants that serve the patrons of the stadium. The income to those businesses on the days immediately before, during, and after stadium events is substantial, and for this reason FPI is able to lease commercial space at a premium price ($40/square foot). Each of the three city blocks has about 100,000 square feet of commercial space.

The current stadium has been in this location for nearly twenty-five years. It is owned and operated by the county (Cala County), and there has been talk regarding the need for a larger and newer facility (particularly for football games). It would be to your company's advantage if the stadium were to remain at its current location, because the leasing value of the properties that you own could drop as much as 50 percent without the stadium.

Alpha Sports Group is the sports management team that owns the football team, the Cobras. They are interested in talking to you about a possible purchase of some of your property. The city block immediately adjacent to the stadium is probably worth around $25 million, in your estimation. The next two city blocks that you own are worth about $12 million each. The new stadium will require about one city block (plus parking).

There is some interest in your company becoming a partner with a major sports team in the area, as generally these are rather profitable enterprises. Not only do they turn a handsome profit (estimated at around 10 percent of gross), but the value of a team on the open market has doubled in the past four years. The team represented by Alpha Sports Group has a long history of success, but in recent years the team's performance and attendance have tailed off. This may be due to a variety of factors, including the retirement of the head coach who built the team, and to greater competition for discretionary dollars (that is, other sporting and entertainment events in the region).

Cala County Government
Confidential Information

You represent the interests of Cala County, a county adjacent to the heart of a major metropolitan area. Cala County consists primarily of residential neighborhoods. However, there is a county-owned stadium located on one edge of the county (closest to the downtown area), which has been the home of the area's major sports team, the Cobras. This football team has played its home games in this stadium since the stadium was first constructed twenty-five years ago. The football team leases the current stadium for $10 million per year, and half of that goes toward maintenance.

The stadium was once considered one of the finest in the league. However, it now lacks many of the amenities of newer stadiums. The owners of the football team that play its games at the stadium, Alpha Sports Group, are most concerned about the lack of capacity and absence of luxury suites, for which major corporations will pay substantial money. The current capacity of the stadium is around 50,000 people. They would like to have a larger stadium, which will take up about a city block.

There are, without question, some major advantages of having the team remain within the county, whether they stay in this stadium or move to another. One advantage is the jobs that are provided by a major sports team. In addition to the 1,000 people that work the stadium, there are shops and restaurants in the area that fans patronize, which also provide jobs (estimated at 800). For every job that is provided, the county earns about 2 percent in tax revenues. While the average salary is relatively low (about $15,000), some of those jobs (most of the 1,000 and approximately 40 percent of the 800) would be lost if the team relocated outside the county. Furthermore, sales tax from the stores in and around the stadium amounts to as much as $200,000 annually (although this has declined about 30 percent in recent years with the team's poor performance).

Over the years, the county has found some additional uses for its stadium, although Alpha Sports Group has lobbied against other events occurring at the stadium during its team's season. However, musical events, circus shows, and a county fair have been scheduled over the years, and these have brought in an increasing revenue stream, reaching as much as $4 million. If the football team were to move, it might be possible to schedule some additional events. While it has been estimated that this would bring in perhaps an additional $750,000, the county would obviously prefer to keep the football team. The football team's lease with the county for use of the stadium expires in three years.

Without a football team or a major sports team of some type, it would not be in Cala County's best interest to build a new stadium. Most of the non-football events function quite well in the current stadium. Although twenty-five years old, the stadium is still structurally sound. However, if a new stadium were built, construction would take a minimum of 18 months and cost as much as $200 million to build.

Index

Abernathy, Ralph, on the future, *ix*
Active leverage, 11, 12, 18, 34, 36, 37
Acxiom Corporation, 46
address, mode of, 28
advertising, 48, 50
affiliation needs
   countermeasure for, 95–96
   to increase your leverage, 49–51
Afghanistan invasion, 4, 180
age, as indicator of leverage, 29
agents for negotiation, 123–124
agreements
   authorship of, 30
   costs of not having, 4–5, 87–88
   leverage and, 3–4
airline strikes, 4–5
Albright, Madeline, 175
Alexander, Jason, 167
Allen, Woody, on show business, 21, 23
Alliance for Progress program, 180
alliances, 97
altering leverage
   choosing approach for, 81–85
   countermeasures for, 93–106
   by decreasing other party's leverage, 55–65
   by increasing your leverage, 45–53
   selecting approach for, 115–120
   test scenarios for, 67–79
altering perceived wants/needs
   countermeasure for, 94–95
   to increase your leverage, 47–49
alternatives
   creating, 61–63, 103–104
   discrediting, 51–52, 96
   eliminating, 52–53, 96–98
   feigning, 63–64
   focusing on, 60
   as source of leverage, 16–17
Ancier, Garth, 167
Annie Get Your Gun (musical), 192
appearance, as indicator of leverage, 29
Apple Records, 62
"The Apprentice" (television show), 26–27
Archimedes, on leverage, 121
Argentina, 179
attire, as indicator of leverage, 25
auctions, 97–98, 106
audit, leverage, 87–88
Australia, 178
authority limits technique, 123
authorship of agreement, 30

Bacon, Francis, on opportunities, 195
balancing leverage, 192–193
Balzac, Honoré de, on revealing power, 67
Barksdale, James, on salesmen, 143, 145
baseball umpire resignations, 62
Beatles, 62
Behavioral Tacit communication, 126, 127, 135, 138
Being There (movie), 12, 13
Bernstein, Carl, 4
bilateral negotiation, 162, 165–170
Blind leverage, 11–13, 17–18, 36, 37
Brazil, 186
Burlington Northern Santa Fe railroad, 62
Bush, George W., 50, 122
buyer's market, 61

Canada, 178, 183–184
canceling meetings, 24–25
CARICOM, 184
Carter, Jimmy, 60
Cheney, Dick, 122
Chesterfield, Lord, on pleasing people, 115
China, 182, 184
Chirac, Jacques, 117
Clark, James, 145
Clemens, Roger, 22, 23, 31
climate of negotiation, creating, 109–113
Clinton, Bill, 50
closure stage, 2, 22
coalitions, 166–167
colleagues, leverage and number of, 27
Columbus, Christopher, 16
communication
  choosing medium for, 124
  face-to-face, 124–127
  levels of interaction in, 125–129
  through agent, 123–124
company stores, 52
competitors, identifying, *see* identifying competitors
consumer base, in international negotiations, 184–185
contact, initiation of, 21–23
Corneille, Pierre, on giving, 191
costs
  determiners of, 15
  hiding/limiting, 13
  leverage and, 4–5
  perceived, 7–8
  potential, 14
  relative, 140–141
countermeasure(s) in negotiation, 93–106
  for altering your perceived wants/needs technique, 94–95
  for creating viable alternatives technique, 103–104
  for discrediting your alternatives technique, 96
  for eliminating your alternatives technique, 96–98
  for feigning disinterest in your product/service technique, 98–99
  for feigning other options technique, 104–106
  for identifying deficiencies in your product/service technique, 99–100
  for identifying your competitors technique, 101–103
  for matching his products/services to your wants/needs technique, 93–94
  for tapping your affiliation needs technique, 95–96
  when other party expands purpose of their pursuit, 100–101
Cousins, Norman, on wisdom, 1
creating alternatives
  countermeasure for, 103–104
  to decrease counterpart's leverage, 61–63
Cuba, 189
culture
  age/gender and leverage in, 29
  and expression of emotions, 154
  and gift-giving, 31–32
  and hierarchy of needs, 19
  in international negotiations, 185–189
customs, differences in, 145
cyberspace, negotiating in, 157–160

Day, Clarence, on experience, 157
DC Partners of Brasalia, 185–186
deception, 144
decreasing other party's leverage, 55–65
  by creating viable alternatives, 61–63
  by expanding purpose of your endeavor, 59–60
  by feigning disinterest in counterpart's product/service, 55–57
  by feigning other options, 63–64
  by identifying counterpart's competitors, 61
  by identifying product/service deficiencies, 57–58
Deep Throat, 4
defensive techniques, *see* countermeasure(s) in negotiation
deficiencies, identifying, *see* identifying deficiencies technique
Detecting Lies and Deceit (A. Vrij), 107
detrimental reliance, 73
"Diplomacy" game, 176
discrediting alternatives
  countermeasure for, 96
  to decrease counterpart's leverage, 51–52
dishonest behavior, detecting, 107, 147–148
disinterest, feigning, *see* feigning disinterest technique
distance
  and leverage, 5, 121–125
  means of achieving, 123–124
Douglas, Norman, on advertisements, 177
dress, style of, 25

Index

Dutch auctions, 98
dynamic leverage, 8–9

economic system, in international negotiations, 183–184
Edison, Thomas, 51
Egypt, 179
electronic mail, 124, 125, 157–159
eliminating alternatives
  countermeasure for, 96–98
  to decrease counterpart's leverage, 52–53
  ethical issue with, 146
e-mail, *see* electronic mail
emotional intelligence, 153–154, 156
emotions
  managing, 151–155
  in negotiation, 1, 2
encounter stage, 2, 22, 31
England, Queen of, 28
Enron, 166
Equatorial Guinea, 179
ethics, 143–148
  and deception, 144
  and differing customs, 145
  and fraud, 144
  managing, 146–148
European Union, 184
exchange rates, 183
exchange stage, 2, 22
expanding purpose technique
  countermeasure for, 100–101
  to decrease other party's leverage, 59–60
Explicit Interaction, 125, 126, 134–135, 138
eye contact, as indicator of leverage, 27

face-to-face communication, 124–129
Federal Bureau of Investigation (FBI), 111–112
feigning disinterest technique
  countermeasure for, 98–99
  to decrease other party's leverage, 55–57
  ethical issue with, 146
feigning other options technique
  countermeasure for, 104–106
  to decrease other party's leverage, 63–64
  ethical issue with, 146
Felt, W. Mark, 4
focus on item, as indicator of interest, 56
Franklin, Benjamin, on necessity, 15
fraud, 144
"Friends" (television show), 167, 193
fulcrum, 5
future opportunities, presenting, 48–49

Galsworthy, John, on men of action, 39
Galtieri, Leopoldo, 173
gender
  and emotional intelligence, 154
  as indicator of leverage, 29
geography, in international negotiations, 179–180
gifts
  as indicator of leverage, 25–26, 31–32
  in international negotiations, 186–187
good guy–bad guy technique, 123

Harrison, George, 28
Hawaii, 180
Henie, Sonja, 3–4
Henry VIII, King of England, 61–62
Heslin, Richard, 32
hierarchy of needs, 19
history, in international negotiations, 180–181
Hodgetts, Richard, 53
Hoffman, Dustin, 137, 141
Holiday Inn, 63
Hoover, J. Edgar, 111–113
Houston Astros, 22, 31
Houston Power & Lighting Company, 62
humor, 50
hurricane Katrina, 148–149

identifying competitors technique
  countermeasure for, 101–103
  to decrease counterpart's leverage, 61
identifying deficiencies technique
  countermeasure for, 99–100
  to decrease other party's leverage, 57–58
identifying leverage, 33–37
Implicit communication, 126, 127, 138
increasing your leverage, 45–53
  by altering counterpart's perceived wants/needs, 47–49
  by discrediting counterpart's alternatives, 51–52
  by eliminating counterpart's alternatives, 52–53
  and maintaining good relationships, 117–119
  by matching product/service to counterpart's wants/needs, 45–47
  by tapping affiliation needs, 49–51
India, 184
indicator(s) of leverage, 21–32
  age as, 29
  appearance as, 29
  author of agreement as, 30
  buying of meals as, 26

indicator(s) of leverage (*continued*)
  contact initiation as, 21–23
  eye contract as, 27
  gender as, 29
  gifts as, 25–26
  interruptions as, 27–28
  language spoken as, 28
  meeting location as, 23–24
  modes of address as, 28
  multiple, 30–31
  number of colleagues as, 27
  order and amount of speaking as, 28
  response time as, 30
  seating arrangement as, 26
  space and posture as, 26–27
  style of dress as, 25
  touching as, 27
  wait time as, 24–25
information, power of, 8–9
international negotiation, 177–189
  and consumer base, 184–185
  and control of natural resources, 178–179
  and culture, 185–189
  and economy, 183–184
  and geography, 179–180
  and history, 180–181
  and legal system, 183–184
  and technology/labor force, 181–183
interruptions, as indicator of leverage, 27–28
Iraq, 171, 179

Jackson, Michael, 27
Japan, 178, 182, 183, 185, 187
Jerusalem, 180–181
Jobs, Steve, 48
Johnson, Lyndon, 113
Jong, Erica, on risk, 137, 141
Jordan, Michael, 195

Kennedy, John, 111–112, 176, 180
Kerry, John, 122
Kissinger, Henry, 176
Kramer vs. Kramer (movie), 137, 141
Kuwait, 179

labor force, in international negotiations, 181–183
language
  leverage and choice of, 28
  in multilateral negotiation, 172
Latin America, 187, 189
Lebowitz, Fran, on polite conversation, 81
legal system, in international negotiations, 183–184

Leonsis, Ted, 195
leverage
  Active, 11, 12, 18, 34, 36, 37
  based on perceptions, 7–8
  Blind, 11–13, 17–18, 36, 37
  consequences of forms of, 109
  definitions of, 2–3
  and distance, 121–125
  distance in, 5
  dynamic nature of, 8–9
  emotion-based, 155
  examples of, 3–4
  perceptions as basis of, 23, 31
  Potential, 13–14, 19, 25
  as situation-specific, 9
  social, 3
  as social or relational construct, 9
  surrendering, 191–193
  and understanding of costs, 5
  Unknown, 14, 19
leverage audit, 87–88
levour, 3
Lincoln, Abraham, 172–173
LinkedIn, 175
Littlefield, Warren, 167
Louise-Dreyfus, Julia, 167
Lovitz, Jon, 105
lowballing, 103
Luthans, Fred, 53

MAD (Mutual Assured Destruction) policy, 93
Madonna, 28
Mafia game, 149, 199–201
Major, Brenda, 32
managers, successful, 53
managing leverage
  methods for, 45
  questionnaire on, 39–43
Marx, Groucho, on belonging to clubs, 55
"M*A*S*H" (television show), 175–176
Maslow, Abraham, 19
McDonald's, 51, 63
McLane, Drayton, 22
meal-buying, as indicator of leverage, 26
mechanical leverage, 2, 3
meetings
  canceling, 24–25
  leverage and location of, 23–24
mercantilism, 53
MERCOSUR, 184
mergers, 97
Mexico, 183–184
Microsoft, 96–98
Middle East, 187

Index

Miller, Zell, 122
mode of address, as indicator of leverage, 28
Montgomery, Colin, 122–123
Morgan, Frank, 30
multilateral negotiation, 162, 170–175
multiparty negotiation, 161–175
  bilateral, 162, 165–170
  levels of complexity in, 163–164
  multilateral, 162, 170–175
  three-party, 203–208
Mutual Assured Destruction (MAD) policy, 93

Nader, Ralph, 166
NAFTA, *see* North American Free Trade Agreement
natural resources, in international negotiations, 178–179
needs
  affiliation, 49–51, 95–96
  Maslow's hierarchy of, 19
  perceived, altering, 47–49
  perceived, matching product/service to, 45–47
  wants vs., 59–60
negative reinforcement, 110–111
negotiation, 1–2
  comparing approaches to, 81–85
  countermeasures in, 93–106
  creating climate of, 109–113
  in cyberspace, 157–160
  emotions in, 152–155
  indicators of leverage in, 21, 22, 31
  international, 177–189
  multiparty, 161–175
  as multistage process, 1, 2
  selecting approach for, 115–120
  stages of, 2, 21, 22
  successful, 121
  testing skills for, 87–91, 131–136
  three-party, 203–208
  through agent, 123–124
  time element in, 53, 63
  uncertainty and risk in, 137–141
  women in, 29
negotiation techniques questionnaire, 39–43
The Netherlands, 179, 181
Netscape, 98
neutralizing parties, 172
Nixon, Richard, 4
Nordstrom's, 148
Normal Trade Relations (NTR), 184, 189
North, Oliver, 27

North American Free Trade Agreement (NAFTA), 183–184
North Korea, 189
NTR, *see* Normal Trade Relations
number of calls/visits, as indicator of interest, 56
number of colleagues, as indicator of leverage, 27

O'Casey, Sean, on losing your temper, 151
office appearance, as indicator of leverage, 25
Olympic Games, 116–117, 181
omission technique, 112
open-ended questions, 46–47
options, feigning, *see* feigning other options technique

pace, as indicator of interest, 56
Pakistan, 4, 180
Panama Canal, 180
Partners of the Americas, 185–186
perceived wants and needs
  altering, 47–49, 94–95
  matching products/services to, 45–47, 93–94
  as most common focus in leverage, 118
perception
  of advantages/disadvantages, 12–13
  as basis of leverage, 7–8, 17, 23
  of emotions, 155
Perot, Ross, 166
political parties, 166, 171
positive reinforcement, 110, 111
post-negotiation stage, 2, 22
posture
  as indicator of leverage, 26–27
  "reading," 147
Potential leverage, 13–14, 19, 25
pre-negotiation stage, 2, 22
price fixing, 52
Prisoner's Dilemma game, 165–166
products
  feigning disinterest in, 55–57
  identifying deficiencies in, 57–58
  matching perceived wants/needs and, 45–47
Publilius Syrus, on mental "seeing," 11
punishment techniques, 111
purpose, expanding, *see* expanding purpose technique

questionnaire (negotiation techniques), 39–43
questions, eliciting wants/needs with, 46–47

Reagan, Ronald, 62
reciprocal behavior, 112–113
reflective inquiries, 47
relational construct, leverage as, 9
relationship building, 95, 117
relative costs, 140–141
Reprise Records, 62
Republican National Convention, 2004, 122
response time, as indicator of leverage, 30
Richards, Michael, 167
risk, 137–141
Rogers, Will, on diplomacy, 93
Rolling Stones, 60
Roosevelt, Franklin, 111
Rosenkrantz, Stuart, 53
Russia, 185
Ryze, 175

Saudi Arabia, 178, 179
Sculley, John, 48
seating arrangement, as indicator of leverage, 26
"Seinfeld" (television show), 8, 105, 166, 167
Sellers, Peter, 12
seller's market, 61
services
    feigning disinterest in, 55–57
    identifying deficiencies in, 57–58
    matching perceived wants/needs and, 45–47
"Sex and the City" (television show), 45–46
Shaw, George Bernard, on breeding, 109
Shedd, John A., on safety, 87
silence, as negotiating tool, 47
Simpson, O.J., 27
Sinai negotiations, 60
Sinatra, Frank, 62
situation specific, leverage as, 9
"60 Minutes" (television show), 29, 57
social construct, leverage as, 9
social leverage, 3, *see also* leverage
social-network services (Internet), 175
Somers, Suzanne, 166, 167
sources of leverage, 15–19
South Africa, 178
Soviet Union, 181, 182, 185
space
    as indicator of leverage, 26–27
    in international negotiations, 187

speaking, leverage and order/amount of, 28
stakeholders in negotiations, 162–163
style of dress, as indicator of leverage, 25
Sun Valley Serenade (movie), 3–4
supply and demand, 16–17
"sweeteners," 13–14, 50

tapered integration, 63
technology, in international negotiations, 181–183
three-party negotiation, 203–208
"Three's Company" (television show), 166, 167
titles, as indicators of leverage, 28
Tom Sawyer, on whitewashing fences, 45, 47
touching, as indicator of leverage, 27
Trotsky, Leon, on beliefs, 7
Trump, Donald, 26–27
Twain, Mark, 47
two-party negotiations, 161

uncertainty, 137–141
Union Pacific railroad, 62
United States, 180, 182–184, 186
Unknown leverage, 14, 19
Uruguay GATT negotiations, 164

Valentino, Michael, 9–10
Verbal Tacit communication, 125–127, 135
videoconferencing, 124
voice mail, 125
Vrij, A., 107

wait time, as indicator of leverage, 24–25
Wall Street Journal, 9–10
Wal-Mart, 62
wants
    altering, 47–49
    matching product/service to, 45–47
    needs vs., 59–60
    as source of leverage, 16–17
Washington Wizards, 195
Wendy's, 51
Wilde, Oscar, on mistakes, 33
The Wizard of Oz (movie), 23–24, 30
women
    and emotional intelligence, 154
    in negotiations, 29
    networking by, 169
Woodward, Bob, 4

Zanuck, Darryl, 3